RENEWING YOUR MIND

Transforming Your Understanding of Who You Are

DAVID VAN TRUMP

© 2016 David Van Trump

All rights reserved. No portion of this book may be reproduced, stored in a retrieval system, or transmitted in any form or by any means–electronic, mechanical, photocopy, recording, scanning, or other–without the prior written permission from the publisher.

Unless otherwise noted, all Scripture quotations are taken from the Holy Bible, New International Version®, NIV®. Copyright © 1973, 1978, 1984, 2011 by Biblica, Inc.® Used by permission of Zondervan. All rights reserved worldwide.

Scripture quotations marked KJV are taken from the King James Version of the Bible.

Scriptures quotations marked ESV are taken from the English Standard Version. © 2001 by Crossway Bibles, a division of Good News Publishers.

Cover Design: Camille Block
Book Design: Camille Block
Images: © Dollar Photo Club

ISBN 978-0-9949665-0-6

Printed in Canada by Kettle Valley Graphics.
First Edition 2016

This book is dedicated to my Dad, Leonard Trump, who passed away peacefully on December 22 2015. Thank you for teaching me all of your valuable lessons in life. I will never forget your bravery and guidance. May peace and love never leave your side.

- David Van Trump

WORDS

Words spoken in pain
Are no words at all

Words spoken in pain
How vain

Death, is what I hear
Why speak at all

Words, words speak life
Words speak death

Words, actions, experiences, love
Those words, do they flow (?)

Or do you experience the worlds
ebbs and flow

Does your world bring you life
Or leave you broken

Where do you reside
Or do you always run and hide

If love knocked on your door
Would you open
Or would you not hear
and remain broken

You were chosen for life
In an unending ocean

Love will keep you afloat
When you are ready, to jump off the boat

CONTENTS

Chapter 1: Importance of Completeness — 1
- Being Complete ... 4
- Religious Misinterpretations ... 10
- Biblical Examples of Fullness ... 14
- Personal Lessons of Miscommunication ... 22

Chapter 2: Transformation — 30
- Personal Experiences with Renewing my Mind ... 34
- The Mind ... 39
- Positive Thinking vs. Renewing Your Mind ... 42
- Band-Aid Renewal ... 48

Chapter 3: Power of Thoughts — 56
- Perception ... 63
- Importance of Balance ... 66
- Proper Balance Brings Rest ... 72

Chapter 4: Power of Emotions — 77
- Negative Thoughts vs. Negative Emotions ... 83
- Personal Lessons from Renewing my Mind ... 88
- Importance of Renewed Emotions ... 94
- Causes of a Negative Emotional State ... 98
- Effects of Pain ... 106
- Personal Experiences with Pain ... 116
- Look to Jesus ... 119

Chapter 5: Forgiveness — 125
    God's Forgiveness First 130
    Forgiving Ourselves vs. Forgiving Others 132

Chapter 6: Iniquity — 140
    Can Bad Things Happen to Good People 143
    A Place of Exchange 148
    Iniquity Exchange 150
    Fully God, Fully Man 158
    Justice 167

Chapter 7: Believing — 172
    Decreasing Doubt 180
    Acceptance 186
    Chastisement 189
    Focus 194
    Moving Jesus into our Hearts 213
    The Fruit of Love 220

Chapter 8: Restoration — 234

End Notes 248

IMPORTANCE *of* COMPLETENESS

CHAPTER 1

All of us love the feeling of being complete. Whether it comes to our jobs, our goals, or our relationships, we all love the feeling of completeness. It makes us feel accomplished, worthy, whole, and valued, like we have all that we need in regards to a particular area. I always remember the feeling of a clean room. If you ask my parents, this was definitely not one of my strong suits. But I am glad they always encouraged me to take care of my surroundings. Needless to say, it usually took me a little longer to complete the task than it did for my siblings. That being said, maybe it allowed me to enjoy the final product all the more.

I would always look at the mess and think to myself, that's going to take way too much effort and time to complete the task. However, on the days that I did find enough motivation to get started, there was no stopping me. Once I was a few minutes into the job, I actually started to enjoy myself. I would usually start with the big stuff that was on the floor. I usually had clothes lying around that I had worn to school the week prior. Well at least we will go with a week before. For those that know me personally, it could have been more like a couple of weeks...

For me this clothes part of the process included more than just throwing everything into the wash. I would have to sort out which clothes were dirty and actually needing a wash, which clothes were still wearable, and which clothes were washed but somehow actually never got put into the dresser from the previous room cleaning experience. I'm sure my parents and future wife will be thanking God everyday for the improved habits I gained over the many years of growing up.

On with my story... After finishing all the big stuff that was lying around, I would move on to cleaning up any shelves, including the top of my dresser. I would begin by throwing out the big items such as papers from school. I would then return any items that I had taken from elsewhere in the house back to their rightful spots. Next, I would organize and arrange the things that I wanted to keep easy access to. After I felt like I was happy with how the shelves and the top of my dresser looked, I would then move on to vacuuming the floor. That sums up most of the process that I can remember.

There were always a couple things that I noticed each time I cleaned my room. The first was a feeling of getting a second wind or a sense of inspiration. I would often go from being hesitant and wanting to avoid cleaning my room, to going through the motions of cleaning, to hitting this cleaner superhero that existed inside of me. This so called superhero seemed to just come out of nowhere and want to clean everything in sight until the job was done perfectly. Looking back on it I see that I just needed a bit of a start. Once I finally got rolling I actually wanted to increase the cleanliness goal that I had originally started with. Also, getting to the finish line seemed to require less effort than taking the first initial steps did.

It reminds me of the saying which goes, "it is easier to move or change an object's course once it is in motion." I think this is a great saying. The first step in something is always the hardest step. Once you are moving towards where you want to end up, you are closer to getting there. If you change your mind and want to go somewhere else, you can still do that just as easily.

The second thing I noticed, which is why I started to tell this story in the first place, was what I felt like inside at the very end once my room was clean, and my task was fully complete. I felt a sense of gratification, happiness, honor, value, and peace. I am sure you can relate to the feeling of complete satisfaction that comes once you complete a meaningful task.

All of us enjoy and desire this feeling of complete satisfaction. The more often we feel and experience this sense of completion, the happier we are in life. When we feel this in our jobs, in our relationships, and in the things we hold most dear to us, we feel amazing about ourselves. The more we can experience this feeling in as many areas of our life that we can, the happier we become. It's not hard to see that this is something that we all want and long for.

The more important question is how do we get it? How do we feel more complete about ourselves in all the areas of our life? Maybe you have thought about this question before, or maybe you think about it all the time. If this sounds like you, then you have come to the right place. I hope to enable you to discover the answer to this question and much more.

BEING COMPLETE

I looked up some of the other words used to describe completeness. The ones that stood out to me were fullness, entirety, totality, and wholeness.[1] Some antonyms for completeness are: lack, void, want, and emptiness. When I think about my life, and all the different parts to it that make me feel love, I desire fullness in all of them, especially in my relationships. When I think about being with someone in a romantic relationship, it makes me cringe thinking about how

I feel inside when our connection is not fully complete. To demonstrate the importance of completeness even further, I want to share a story.

There once was a man who suddenly loses his job and gets evicted from his house. He decides to sell all of his clothes except for his one favorite outfit. He then goes to the bank and takes out the rest of the money that he possesses. He has enough to buy breakfast and dinner for the next three months, but has to live under a bridge as he does not have enough money to get a place to stay. A few days into this new life of his he spots a jacket that is just sitting there on a park bench with no owner in sight. He decides to keep an eye on the jacket, and if it is still there the following day he is going to claim it. Sure enough the jacket is still sitting there the following evening and he decides to claim it. He thanks God that he can now sleep a little warmer at night.

A week goes by and he still has not been able to find a job. He goes out every morning to hand out resumes but nothing changes. With his limited budget he can only eat two small meals a day and continue to hope that a job will open up as soon as possible. Three months pass by and still no job. He eats the last meal that he can afford and goes back under the bridge to get ready for bed. He wonders how on earth he is going to be able to survive another day. To his surprise a full week passes by and all he has eaten are the scraps that he finds lying around where he goes.

6

That night he is not able sleep with all the fear and worry running through his mind. He decides to go sit on the park bench where he found the coat months back. A rush of emotion floods his entire body and he has to put his hands over his face to cover all of his tears. He decides that in the morning he will sell the jacket and use whatever money he gets from it to buy food for as long as he can. The feeling of starvation far outweighs the thought of freezing to death as he sleeps.

Morning arises and he heads into town making his way to the local thrift shop. He enters the store, takes off the jacket, and waits in line. Finally his turn comes to go up to the counter. He puts on a brave face and answers, "Fine," when the cashier asks him how he is doing. He asks her how much he can get for the jacket.

She responds, "Ten dollars is all I can give you for this."

He accepts the offer and hands over the jacket. He takes the ten dollars from the cashier and heads to the door, all the while thinking about where he can find the cheapest breakfast spot. He opens up the door and walks out into his unknown future. He spots a place across the street where he can purchase a cheap meal. All he can think about is filling the empty void of hunger that exists inside of him. He reaches the corner and waits for the light to turn red so that he can walk across. The time comes for his turn to be allowed to cross the road. He starts his walk across while thinking to himself, "All these people care about is having their turn at the light. I bet most of them are going off to their jobs, driving their kids to school, or heading back home to their families. I have no place to go and no one special to see. I have no one who cares for me."

All of a sudden he hears a lady yelling, "Hey mister!" He turns around and sees the cashier from the thrift shop waving to him. "Hey mister," she yells again. Holding up a white envelope she asks, "Is this yours?" He decides to turn around and go see what she is talking about, and what she is holding in her hand. When he reaches her she says, "I found this in the inner pocket of the jacket you gave me."

Right away he thinks back and remembers the day he saw the jacket sitting on the park bench. He thinks to himself, "Maybe someone left something inside of the jacket. Maybe I can get a hold of them and tell them how I found the jacket." He decides to take the envelope, but before opening it, he decides to head over to the diner to quench the painful hunger he feels inside. After his meal, he decides to open up the letter and look inside. He finds a piece of paper with a note on it, and he begins to read it.

To whom it may concern,

I once lived part of my life homeless and I know the difficulties and struggles one faces on the street. If you are reading this, I have since passed. I have no children of my own, and only a few older friends that live in the area. I decided that it is my wish to leave this jacket, along with my estate, to someone facing the struggles of living on the street. If you find this jacket, please feel free to keep it. On the back side of this page is my signature and bank account number which has all the money I possessed inside. I have arranged with the bank to give the money in the account, along with the title of my home, to the person who comes in with this letter. So for the one who finds this letter, God bless you. I hope you fulfill all the dreams and desires you have in this world.

Now let me get to the point for sharing this story. This man that lived under the bridge for over three months, did he have to experience being homeless and hungry for the entirety of the three months?

The answer is no. He found the jacket a few days after he lost his job and got evicted from his house. At any moment in time between finding the jacket and the cashier giving him the envelope, he could have received the inheritance. He could have been living in a house, eating food, while using the money in the bank account for whatever he desired. So what is the reason he did not experience this sooner in his life?

The reason is because he was not aware of all that was in his possession. What was in the fullness of his possessions was everything that he was aware of plus the letter which he was unaware of. In other words, his awareness of what he had was not full. His awareness in regards to the letter was lacking or void. Do you remember earlier when I described the many words for fullness, and the words that described the opposite of fullness? Lacking and void were among the list of antonyms.

I like this analogy as it really drives home the point of fullness. It really captures the importance of fullness and the dangers of incompleteness. Can you think of any other situations where fullness is so vital, and lack thereof can create undesired situations?

How about having just two numbers to a five coded lock on a safe, which holds precious jewels, diamonds, and gold inside. How about a lack of a complete nutrition. Or maybe even a marriage where one partner doesn't completely know or accept the other person. Now things are getting a little more devastating. I am sure you get my point, that fullness and completeness are very important in many situations and areas of our lives. Or one could say that being void and incomplete are very detrimental to certain situations and areas of our lives.

RELIGIOUS MISINTERPRETATIONS

For this book, I will be focusing on the dangers of being incomplete in key areas of our lives. In this section, I want to discuss the dangers of being incomplete in language. There are many languages in the world, and certain words lose much of their valuable meaning when being translated. Even when a person conceptualizes a written word from a book in the same language, meaning can be lost. What an author tries to portray and explain may get lost when the reader begins to interpret what they are reading.

I am sure you have all experienced this in one sense or another. You may have experienced this while trying to find the right words in another language to try to explain what you want to say. But even within the same language this can occur. This can be experienced when you are communicating with someone and they try to describe something, but you interpret and hear what they are saying in a completely different way. This can often lead to fights and disagreements depending on what you are talking about, and who you are talking with. The same thing can happen when you are reading a book, and you misinterpret what the author is trying to say. Sometimes you may understand part of what the author is trying to say, but you miss out on the other parts that are trying to be portrayed.

Oftentimes you may not understand the full meaning of what is being said, but since the subject matter is not vitally important, no severe consequences result. Since the misinterpretation is not that big of a deal, it often gets cleared up in a matter of time. If you understand it fully, great, if you don't, life will still go on. However, other subject matter can hold a much deeper importance to the reader. The message the author is trying to get across is quite important, and if the reader doesn't fully get the interpretation, it's going to cause major consequences.

I myself like to read the Bible. I believe that the content in the Bible has a very high level of importance in my life. So for me to receive exactly what God is trying to say to me, and to interpret it correctly, is something I truly value. I try as much as possible to not misinterpret what I am reading. I also try not to assume certain things in the Bible when I am reading. That is, I try to avoid thinking that I fully understand a word I am reading about, when in fact I do not. To me, both of these scenarios have dangers that can affect both my life, and those I love around me.

It doesn't take that long of a look back in history to see examples of what I am talking about. I am sure all throughout history people have misinterpreted what was trying to be said in their religion. This is no different with the Bible. Extreme groups of people seem to always exist and are sometimes even willing to die, or kill others, to prove that they are right. Some of these atrocities have been well documented. For example, many women were burned at the stake a few hundred years ago because religious thought claimed that they were witches. Many people believed that it was their responsibility to put them to death because that is what they perceived God wanted them to do. One of the popularized individuals who died as a result of this religious misinterpretation was Joan of Arc, who was executed in the 1400's.

Another example is Galileo Galilei, who was an astronomer in the 16th and 17th centuries. He believed in the heliocentric theory, which states that the earth and the other planets in our solar system revolve around the sun. For us in the 21st century, this is common knowledge, since this was what we learned while going to school. However, people who lived in Galileo's era believed quite the opposite. The common knowledge was that the earth was at the center of the solar system, and that the planets and the sun rotated around it. When this new theory opposed the accepted ideas of that time period, it created quite the controversy. The religious institutions at the time were very threatened by this new idea. They claimed that this new idea went against what was written in the scriptures. Thus, Galileo was regarded as a heretic for his scientific beliefs, and as a result, was opposed by the church.

I am sure there are many more examples throughout history where people have misinterpreted, misused, and misrepresented God's word. Maybe you are familiar with the crusades of long ago. Maybe you have seen more recent examples of what I am talking about which still go on today. I myself am aware of many religious atrocities. It is unfortunate that this sort of thing still occurs in our world today. I don't want to go too far into detail about them in my book however. I just wanted to mention it to draw your attention to the fact that it does exist, and that we must be careful when interpreting scripture. We want to avoid taking things out of context as much as possible. When reading scripture, our goal is to interpret the exact message God is trying to relay to us, nothing more and nothing less. I will share next about the dangers that come when we add on to what God has to say. Later in the book, I will be discussing the dangers of underestimating what God is trying to say. More specifically, the underestimation I find so many people making today regarding one key word.

When something as important as scripture is being interpreted, it is vital that the reader interpret the full meaning out of what is trying to be said. When this fails to happen, it becomes very dangerous, not only for us, but also for others around us. As we just saw, one can easily see the importance of properly interpreting scripture, by either looking back at history, or by looking at our world today. I am sure by now you get the importance of my point. That not understanding and interpreting the fullness of what is written in scripture can lead to fundamental mistakes.

Without completeness we can miss the whole point of a topic. Without completeness, we may not get the results that we desire. When it comes to fullness in the area of faith, I am not sure if anything is more important. Without the fullness of one's faith, the power and miracles talked about in the Bible will never become our experiences here on earth.

BIBLICAL EXAMPLES OF FULLNESS

Even within scripture God shares with us stories that are meant to teach us the importance of fullness. One of the very first things God tries to teach man is the importance of understanding and applying His words fully. What God says out of His mouth is exactly what is. Over the next few points, I want to draw your attention to the vital importance of fullness, or lack thereof, which shows up in the Bible. Moreover, how when God says something, then anything added on to what He says, or anything left off of what He says, is going to have major implications.

God Himself demonstrates the importance of being exact and concise with words in Genesis chapter 1.

And God said, "Let there be light, and there was light."
Genesis 1:3

And God said, "Let the water under the sky be gathered to one place, and let dry ground appear." And it was so.
Genesis 1:9

Then God said, "Let us make mankind in our image, in our likeness, so that they may rule over the fish of the sea and the birds in the sky, over the livestock and all the wild animals, and over all the creatures that move along the ground." So God created mankind in his image, in the image of God he created them; male and female he created them.
Genesis 1:26-27

All throughout Genesis chapter 1, when God says something, that is exactly what happens. I believe He is demonstrating the power of His words. If He were to add anything more to what He said, then that would be so. If He were to say, "Let's create three genders, male, female, and something else," then that would have happened. Whatever He said happened. That is why He didn't say lets create three genders, because that would have been so, and that isn't what was in His design to create.

Right away here we can already see the importance of being exact. What He fully said, that is what fully happened. If He would have said anything more or anything less, then that is exactly what would have happened. So we can already see the importance of fullness when it comes to what God says. How about the importance of what we say? If saying something exact is important to God, surely it must also be important for us. Let's take a deeper look. A little later in the book of Genesis we can see the importance of fullness again, this time as it relates to us.

And the Lord God commanded the man, "You are free to eat from any tree in the garden; but you must not eat from the tree of the knowledge of good and evil, for when you eat from it you will certainly die."
Genesis 2:16-17

Here we can see exactly what God fully said to Adam. However, later in chapter 3 we will see the serpent come to Eve. Keep in mind she was not created yet when God gave Adam the command. What you will see is that Eve adds on additional words to what God had spoken to Adam. Because what Eve says isn't fully what God had actually said, both she and Adam become susceptible to the lies of the serpent.

Now the serpent was more crafty than any of the wild animals the Lord God had made. He said to the woman, "Did God really say, 'You must not eat from any tree in the garden'?"

The woman said to the serpent, "We may eat fruit from the trees in the garden, but God did say, 'You must not eat fruit from the tree that is in the middle of the garden, and you must not touch it, or you will die."

"You will not certainly die," the serpent said to the woman. "For God knows that when you eat from it your eyes will be opened, and you will be like God, knowing good and evil."
Genesis 3:1-5

Do you see the part Eve added on to in regards to what God had told Adam? God told Adam not to eat of the tree. But Eve tells the serpent that God told them not to eat of it, and not to touch it. In other words, what Eve tells the serpent isn't fully what God had said. She adds on to the fullness of what was said before, and like I mentioned earlier, taking away parts of fullness, or adding on additional things to fullness, is very problematic. In this case it had vital consequences.

So here is what I believe happened. God never told Adam that he could not touch the fruit from the tree of the knowledge of good and evil. He only told Adam when you eat from it you will die. But Eve adds on to the fullness of God's words and says that they also are not allowed to touch it. She thinks that God said if you touch it you will die. So the enemy convinces Eve to touch the fruit. Eve touches it and sees that nothing happens to her, she never dies. So she thinks to herself, "If God said we would die when we touch it, and I just touched it and never died, then that must mean God is lying to us. He must also be lying to us about eating the fruit and dying." So she then decides to eat the fruit and give some to Adam to eat. We all know the story from here. Right after this we read about them feeling naked and ashamed, and hiding from God. Adam and Eve went from feeling complete and communing with God, to feeling ashamed and hiding from Him. I believe if Eve would have responded to the serpent with the exact words that God had spoken to Adam about not eating from the tree, they would not have been deceived. However, this wasn't the case, she added on extra words to what God had said, and the rest is history.

The dangers of adding on to God's words are obvious. Not only did it affect Adam and Eve in the garden, it also has affected many people throughout history. During my life time I have seen many examples of religious extremists, people who take the words written out of certain books and misinterpret the point, and then behave in a way that is not pleasing to God. We can see this in the news today with what is going on in the Middle East. However, this is not just a problem with certain religions. I have seen it done in all of them, including Christianity. People killing abortion doctors because they don't believe in abortion, and they believe that God told them to do it, or that what they read in the Bible tells them to carry out such actions. This adding on to scriptures fullness, and misinterpreting what God is trying to convey, often ends up resulting in extremely dangerous actions. It's not hard to see the dangers of this played out in our world. Like I mentioned earlier, I am sure that you yourselves can come up with many more examples where you see this occurring.

Satan even tried to deceive Jesus with this idea of questioning what God had actually said. We see a clear example of this is the book of Mathew; more specifically in Mathew chapter 3 where we read about Jesus' baptism.

And when Jesus was baptized, immediately he went up from the water, and behold, the heavens were opened to him, and he saw the Spirit of God descending like a dove and coming to rest on him; and behold, a voice from heaven said, "This is my beloved Son, with whom I am well pleased."
Mathew 3:16-17 (ESV)

After this event, we read that Jesus was led by the Spirit into the wilderness to be tempted. We read that Jesus fasted for forty days and forty nights, and He became hungry. We read next that the tempter shows up to test Jesus. What strikes me right away is the first thing that he says to Jesus.

And the tempter came and said to him, "If you are the Son of God, command these stones to become loaves of bread."
Mathew 4:3 (ESV)

Before, during Jesus' baptism, we hear heaven open up and God say, "This is my beloved Son!" All of a sudden Satan shows up and purposely leaves out the beloved part, only saying Son of God, rather than the beloved Son of God. Jesus could have easily answered him with, "It was just said to me a little while ago that I am the beloved Son of God." But He chooses to answer him differently. I believe this is done to teach us how to respond back to the devil when he comes to tempt us.

If you read on in chapter 4, Jesus always answers the devil with the phrase, 'it is written.'

Jesus answered, "It is written: 'Man shall not live on bread alone, but on every word that comes from the mouth of God.'"

Then the devil took him to the holy city and had him stand on the highest point of the temple. "If you are the Son of God," he said, "throw yourself down. For it is written: "'He will command his angels concerning you, and they will lift you up in their hands, so that you will not strike your foot against a stone.'"

Jesus answered him, "It is also written: 'Do not put the Lord God to the test.'"

Again, the devil took him to a very high mountain and showed him all the kingdoms of the world and their splendor. "All this I will give you," he said, "if you will bow down and worship me."

Jesus said to him, "Away from me, Satan! For

it is written: 'Worship the Lord your God, and serve him only.'"

Then the devil left him, and angels came and attended him.
Mathew 4:4-11

Jesus knew exactly how to interpret scripture. He knew when the devil was trying to get Him to see a scripture out of context, and we see that He responded back with another scripture. Jesus knew the importance of properly interpreting the scriptures to exactly what God had intended when He said them. He knew the dangers of adding on meaning, or of subtracting meaning, when it came to interpreting scripture.

When God says something, then that is the way it is. It is extremely important to not change anything that He has said. His Word is superior above all else. In the book of Revelation, God states the importance of exactness in regards to what was said in this chapter. We see this in Revelation 22:18-19.

I warn everyone who hears the words of the prophecy of this book: if anyone adds to them, God will add to him the plagues described in this book, and if anyone takes away from the words of the book of this prophecy, God will take away his share in the tree of life and in the holy city, which are described in this book.
Revelation 22:18-19 (ESV)

It is clear here of the importance of what was written. Anything added, or anything taken away, is not going to be a good thing.

For the other books of the Bible, it is also very important to know exactly what God is saying. We never want to read a scripture and think it means one thing, when in fact it means something else. The goal of reading scripture is to get the exact message God is trying to tell us. I am sure everyone can think of at least one religious atrocity that has occurred as a result of someone not receiving the exact message God was trying to tell them as they were reading.

In any relationship it is important to properly interpret what the other person is trying to say. Whether you are listening to someone, or reading about someone, proper interpretation in regards to understanding the exact message they are trying to convey to you is key; any breakdown in communication, whether it is adding on meaning, or taking away meaning to a phrase or word that someone else is trying to say, will result in disconnection.

PERSONAL LESSONS OF MISCOMMUNICATION

I want to share a true story of how God showed me the importance of hearing what He has to say in His word, versus what I thought He meant. It occurred when I first believed in God and was learning more about Him. That day I was reading Genesis chapter 1. I remember the first scripture that came to life for me, it was Genesis 1:1.

In the beginning God created the heavens and the earth.
Genesis 1:1

I was so happy when I received that, it felt like I knew a truth inside of me that no one could ever take away. I continued reading and had never been happier in my life. I got to Genesis 1:3.

And God said, "Let there be light," and there was light. God saw that the light was good, and he separated the light from the darkness.
Genesis 1:3-4

I remember saying to myself, "Ok, so God thinks everything that is white is good, and everything that is black is bad." Can you already see my error? Anyways, I kept reading, and I got all the way to Genesis 1:24 where God talks about how He created the livestock, the creatures that move along the ground, and all the animals. At this exact moment I looked down on my bed and saw my cat lying there. My cat is mostly black...

All of a sudden I felt a wave of confusion come over me. I thought to myself, "I can't trust in this Bible. God just told me to hate everything that is black, and now I am looking at my cat who I know from my life experiences that I love very dearly." I thought to myself, "I'm sorry, I'm going to stick with what I know and love from my life experiences. I'm not listening to what the Bible has to say if it's telling me to hate all things that are black." I know this sounds very funny reading it, but this literally happened to me. It is quite humorous even writing about it and remembering it. However, when I actually experienced this years back, it was very scary and confusing, and it completely rocked everything I knew.

So here I was, completely torn within myself, having to choose to keep listening to what I thought the Bible wanted me to believe, versus what I knew through my life experiences to be true. I remember saying to God, "Sorry I can't believe in you, I'm going to stick with what I know is true from my life. I can't believe in someone that tells me to hate things that are black in color."

Then I heard Him say to me, "Did I say that?"

I responded back, "Uh, yeah! Right here in verse three!!! You created light, and then separated the light from the darkness. So I am sorry, I am not going to hate things that are dark in color!"

Then He said the same thing to me again, "Did I say that?"

I repeated back the same response to Him.

After He politely let me finish, He said the same thing again,

"Did I say that?"

So I repeated the same thing to Him again, "You see right here in verse three, you are telling me to hate things that are dark in color!!!" I remember thinking to myself, "Is He hard of hearing? I have told Him three times now what He has said to me, and He keeps responding back with, did I say that?"

I started to think to myself the words He had just said to me. "Did I say that! Did I say that? What the heck does He mean, did I say that? He keeps saying this phrase to me, and I keep telling Him that He did. What the heck is the deal? I don't get this. Of course He said that, I keep telling Him that." I remember saying out loud, "Hello, where are you God? Do you care to explain why you keep saying, did I say that?"

I was met with silence on His end.

I thought to myself, "This is ridiculous. I must be hearing voices. I keep hearing this voice I have never heard before say to me, did I say that?"

Then, all of a sudden, a light bulb went off inside of me. I remember it hit me like a ton of bricks. I was like, "No, I said that!!! I said that God. I read what was written in verse three, and then I said what it said!!!" It was like a moment of teaching in itself. I was like, "This is what you wrote here in verse three God, and this is what I think it means." In other words, He wrote that He created the light and then separated it from the darkness. What I read and interpreted was that I was responsible for not liking things that are dark in color.

Okay, now this made sense to me. I remember instantly feeling peace again. God was not telling me to hate dark colors. This was just what I was interpreting. What God was trying to say to me was different than what I was conceptualizing. Well that makes sense. Thank goodness too, because I would hate to have to do that!

I remember taking the time right after this experience to stop and reflect on it. I thought to myself, "How silly can I be. How can I read what is in the Bible and make such an obvious mistake of interpretation. C'mon David!!!" How could I have read Genesis 1:3 and think that God was telling me to not like dark colors! That has got to be the silliest, easiest, and worst misinterpretation of scripture of all time. I bet you God is having a good chuckle to Himself over that one. But as funny and silly as this story is, I feel God was allowing me to go through that experience to teach me a valuable lesson. Throughout my entire life, I will never forget that story.

More importantly, I will never forget the lesson I learned that day about reading scripture. That is, I will never allow myself to think I know exactly what God is trying to say to me through His word, without having Him say it to me Himself. What I mean by this is if I am putting my ideas, my opinions, and my connotations on the verses that I am reading, then there is a good chance that I will hear and interpret the verse, or concept, in a way that I desire it to be heard, instead of hearing exactly what God is trying to say and convey to me.

It is my job to pick up the Bible and use my eyes to read what is written on the pages. But it is God's job, through the Holy Spirit, to speak to me the truth of what is being said.

This reminds me of a verse in proverbs 2:6.

For the Lord gives wisdom; from his mouth come knowledge and understanding.
Proverbs 2:6

What jumps out at me when I read this is that from His mouth come knowledge and understanding. Now when something comes out of a mouth, the way we understand it is by listening. So likewise, the way we learn from God is by listening to His scriptures as we read them, not just by simply reading them. Listening is the key.

We even see this idea written about in the Bible. The Pharisees were a group of leaders who read the scriptures more than anyone else. I don't think anyone could have read the scriptures more often than this group of men. However, in the end, when Jesus was crucified, they were part of the group that helped make it happen. How could a group like this, who read the scriptures probably daily, miss the entire point of what they were reading about? The very scriptures they were reading, if they were interpreted correctly, would have lead them straight into seeing that Jesus was the Messiah. I believe part of the reason why they didn't figure this out was because they were too busy reading the scriptures, and less willing to let God tell them about the scriptures. They missed this major key about listening. I believe when a person is set in their ways, they will hear what they want to hear.

Today as Christians, we have been given the Holy Spirit. He is the One who helps us interpret and hear what we are reading. He is the One who guides us into all truth. When we try and read the Bible without the help of the Holy Spirit we will misinterpret the truth God is trying to convey to us. We must also let go of certain preconceived notions we hold while reading. If we come into reading the Bible with a preconceived notion about God, it will be impossible for us to learn new things if that preconception is wrong. So we must be willing to keep an open mind in order to be able to hear God's truth. I remember reading a sign a while back that I liked which was posted on a church's message board that reminds me of this idea. It read, "Don't try and change the word to fit you, let the word change you."

We all know the consequences that can result when scripture is taken out of context. Fortunately for me, in the story I just shared, the only thing that came out of it was a few minutes of complete confusion and disarray. However, as I mentioned earlier, the results can be a lot more catastrophic. Taking scripture out of context is always dangerous and it is something we want to avoid as much as possible.

In the next section of the book I want to share a scripture that I feel as a body of Christ we have not fully understood. This scripture is a very important one, and is one that I hear many Christians quote all the time. I don't think people are wrongly interpreting the scripture and its purpose. However, I do feel that the majority of Christians aren't getting the fullness out of what God is trying to convey. As a result, many Christians who use this scripture are only experiencing part of the benefits God desires them to have. It's not that what they are practically doing with the scripture is wrong, it's more so that they are only using one aspect of it, when God wants us to be using it to its fullness.

As we saw earlier, not getting the fullness out of things can be just as problematic as misinterpretations of scripture. It is my belief that worldly traditions in this area have climbed into the church, and thus limited the power we experience when practically using this particular scripture. I hope by now you can see the utter importance for us in interpreting exactly what God is trying to convey to us. Moreover, how fullness will positively impact our lives.

TRANS-FORM*ation*

CHAPTER 2

Therefore, I urge you, brothers and sisters, in view of God's mercy, to offer your bodies as a living sacrifice, holy and pleasing to God—this is your true and proper worship. Do not conform to the pattern of this world, but be transformed by the renewing of your mind. Then you will be able to test and approve what God's will is—his good, pleasing and perfect will.
Romans 12:1-2

This is now one of my favorite scriptures in the Bible. I have seen God do so many amazing things in my life thus far. But what happened to me at the end of last year seems to stick out the most. I experienced a transformation in my life, which for a long time had been haunting me, and was destroying me from the inside out.

I absolutely love this verse in the Bible. God is telling us that we can be transformed. What's even greater than telling us that we can be transformed, is the fact that He actually tells us how we can achieve it. I mean, who doesn't want transformation in at least one area of their life?

I looked up the word transformation and this is what I found: to make an impactful or drastic change in the form, appearance, or character of something, often implying for the better.[2] How awesome is this scripture; a drastic change in form for the better! So for someone who is sick and has a life threatening disease, God is saying that can be drastically changed. For someone who is addicted to drugs, or alcohol, and notices that it is destroying every relationship that they have, God is saying that also can be drastically changed. For someone facing constant fear, or anxiety, and is never able to move forward and chase after their dreams in life, God is saying that also can be drastically changed. This is amazing! God is telling us that the pattern of being in the world, or being of the world, can be broken.

We don't have to look far to see the truth of this scripture. We only need to look at the life Jesus lived, to see the results.

Jesus was definitely someone who wasn't conformed to the pattern of the world. We see this all throughout the Gospels. The pattern of the world is that when someone dies, they are dead. But Jesus showed us that is not the pattern of His world, when He raised Lazarus from the dead. The pattern of the world is that when someone is blind, they will be blind for the rest of their life. But Jesus showed us that is not the pattern of His world, as He opened many blind eyes. I could write a whole entire book about all the miracles Jesus performed while He was walking the earth. Fortunately we already have the Bible that we can read, if we want to hear all about them.

Jesus proved that His world, His Kingdom, is greater than the actual world. I feel that is why this verse is telling us not to conform to the world we see around us, but to believe in, and to experience life in, His Kingdom. So I ask you, what areas in your life do you wish to have transformed? What areas in life are you not happy with? For myself, I used to struggle with addictions, depression, and anxiety. But today, my new self is completely free from all such things. I believe that whatever your answers are to these questions, God has a solution.

I believe that He wants to take you from exactly right where you are, into a life that your heart desires. I believe God is giving us the practical answer in this verse, as to how to take our life from one place to another. In the areas of our lives that we are unhappy, or unsatisfied with, I believe we can leave those places, and get to the places we dream of. I believe the way to achieve this is by renewing your mind.

Doesn't this sound too simple and easy to be true? So all I need to do is renew my mind and then I will reap benefits from doing that! Can it really be that easy? I believe the answer is, 'basically' yes. I say 'basically' here on purpose, because I believe it all depends on how much one understands what is being said in Romans 12:1-2. That is, how fully one understands this scripture. Hopefully by the end of the book you will understand why I added the 'basically' in front of the yes.

I believe that what a person believes about themselves will come to be in the world. They have made movies and written books about this idea. Most people are familiar with the concept of 'the law of attraction.' If you are not familiar with this law, I am sure you have heard about other people who are really big into positive thinking, or positive affirmations. I believe it is actually a Biblical principle to think positively. We see the importance of such thinking mentioned in Philippians 4:8.

Finally, brothers and sisters, whatever is true, whatever is noble, whatever is right, whatever is pure, whatever is lovely, whatever is admirable—if anything is excellent or praiseworthy—think about such things.
Philippians 4:8

I have had many conversations with people who say they are Christians, and others who say they are atheists, and no matter their belief system, I have heard them mention positive thinking numerous times. I hear the phrase used all of the time by my friends, people I pass on the street, and people I see on television. This idea that says, "I need to think more positively." It's no secret that people almost everywhere believe thinking more positively is beneficial to them. Other people may say something like, "Look on the bright side." No matter where you are from, I am sure you have heard at one point in your life someone say something along these lines. It's common knowledge for a reason. Thinking more positively is something that benefits us, and it is something that we want to do in our lives. You don't need to be a Christian, or be familiar with the words of Philippians 4:8, to understand that positive thinking is beneficial.

But how do we properly do it? If you could just think your way into a better life, then wouldn't everyone already be doing it! Positive thinking, or renewing your mind, is not as simple as repeating thoughts and/or words to yourself over and over again, and expecting your life to change. There is more to it than that. Throughout this book you will learn what else it entails.

PERSONAL EXPERIENCES WITH RENEWING MY MIND

In this section I want to discuss my personal life experiences that I had with positive thinking. I went through a time in life where I definitely needed positivity and a change in my circumstances.

Last year was a great year for me, I chased after a lifelong dream that I had. That process started bringing a deeper sense of satisfaction for me in life. Throughout the year, my relationship with God was continually growing. I was learning new things about Him, and about myself. I signed up for, and completed my first ever class, that was connected to a Bible school. The year had its ups and downs, but all in all, I could see God's hand behind it all. I saw myself constantly growing and maturing, and I was very happy about that. I was the type of person that needed to learn things the hard way. That is, I needed to learn them by experience. Because of this, it got me into trouble, and it also took me longer to figure things out. Nonetheless, I learned what I needed to learn in the end. All in all, it was a great year of growth for me.

Things were looking wonderful for me near the end of the year. I felt like I had gotten out of certain lifestyle choices that I no longer wanted for myself. I was living the life I desired, and I felt like I was heading towards my future dreams and goals. However, last November that all seemed to change for me. I received some news that really hurt and upset me. Before I knew it, all the growth that I thought I had achieved throughout the year went flushing down the drain. I was devastated and hurt. Over the course of the next few weeks, I was right back into living a lifestyle that I didn't desire for myself. I became very depressed and lethargic. It felt like life lost much of its flavor and allure. I questioned my faith and felt like it was pointless.

After a few weeks had passed, I finally got sick and tired of feeling the way that I did. I asked my family and my close friends what I could do to feel better. I felt like nobody had the answer that I needed. I called one of my good friends and he told me that I needed to renew my mind. When he said this, it felt right to me, like this could be my answer.

So I asked him, "How do I do that? How do I renew my mind?"

He responded back by saying, "Whenever a certain thought comes to you that says something that isn't true, then you replace it with a scripture that is true from the Bible."

I thought to myself, okay, I can do this. I had been spending a lot of the year reading my Bible, so I was familiar with quite a few scriptures. I knew the way the thoughts I was thinking was making me feel, and I knew I wanted to change the way I felt. So I began to do what my friend had told me to do.

This is a dialogue that I remember having with myself last year: of thinking certain thoughts, then replacing the thoughts with other positive thoughts. If any of you are familiar with positive thinking, or with the process of renewing your mind, I am sure you can relate.

Thought: "You're no good. You're a terrible person. You're never going to amount to anything in this world."

Myself: "I am a great person. I am going to do amazing things in this world. I was created for greatness."

I remember thinking to myself, "This is great. I finally know what to do. I'm just going to keep renewing my mind every time these thoughts come to me, and before I know it, I will be out of this funk that I am in." So for the rest of that day, anytime negative thoughts came to me, I replaced them with positive ones.

The next day I started the same process again. I went about replacing the negative thoughts with positive ones. Sometime early in the afternoon, I got the idea to start using scriptures as well. I figured if I can think positive thoughts, and back it up with scripture to prove that it is true, then what I am saying is going to have all the more power. I thought to myself, "What a great idea. This is definitely going to work, and before I know it, I will be feeling like myself again."

So there I was, day two. Here is a dialogue that I remember having with myself that day: of thinking certain thoughts, then replacing those thoughts with other positive thoughts backed with scripture.

Thought: "You're no good. You're a terrible person. You're never going to amount to anything in this world."

Myself: "I am a great person. God makes me great. The Bible says Jesus died for me and loves me. I'm going to do amazing things in this world. I can do all things through Christ Jesus who strengthens me. I was created for greatness. God is my Father, He created me. He created me with a purpose, He created me for greatness. His thoughts about me are more numerous than all the sand on the seashores. He knows the exact number of hairs on my head. He knows how great I am and of all the good things that are in store for me in my life."

I remember thinking to myself, "Okay, now the enemy is in trouble. Not only do I recognize the thoughts he's saying to me that aren't true, but now I know what God says about me. Every time I hear thoughts that don't line up with what God says and thinks about me, I am going to replace them with the truth. Before I know it, I will be laughing and right back to feeling great. Then I will be able to get back to living the life I desire."

Time ticked by that day and I kept going about this same process of renewing my mind. I woke up the next day and did the same thing. I remember thinking to myself, "This is great. I'm finally on the right track!" I had just learned about spiritual warfare, in a sermon right before this. In that sermon I learned that the battle is in our minds.

For our struggle is not against flesh and blood, but against the rulers, against the authorities, against the powers of this dark world and against the spiritual forces of evil in the heavenly realms.
Ephesians 6:12

I remember thinking to myself, "I finally know the battle ground and what the enemy is trying to do to me. All of the things I need are included in the finished works of Jesus. I just need to keep renewing my mind, and before I know it, peace will manifest in the natural realm, and I will fully experience it. I just need to keep up with the process of renewing my mind and the transformation from being depressed to becoming peaceful will have no choice but to show up over time."

Let me put this story aside for a little bit and move on to something else. I will come back to this story in chapter 4 and explain exactly what happened to me. Do you think I was able to obtain the peace that I longed for by using these practical steps of positively renewing my mind? Or was I missing a piece of the puzzle that I needed to understand before I could experience my breakthrough? In the next section, I will begin to introduce what I learned from looking back on this whole experience.

THE MIND

If you are familiar with the process of renewing your mind, I am sure this is what you have also been told to do. In fact, every time I go to a church, or hear a sermon online about renewing the mind, this is exactly what I hear pastors tell their congregation to do. I don't believe this process of renewing your mind is wrong. I just believe this process of renewing your mind, in this exact way, is incomplete. If you remember earlier, in the chapters before, I talked about the dangers of being incomplete. Fullness is what we desire as believers, and without the fullness of something, there is a void.

I don't say my steering wheel in my car, is my car. Or that my gas pedal in my car, is my car. Nor do I say that my tires are my car. All of these things make up my car, as well as many other pieces. But in and of themselves, they are not my car. My car is an accumulation of all the parts inside and out, which complete it. Take any part out of my car and it loses part of its function. Some functions are more important than others. If you take out my stereo system, I can still get to and from my destination, just without music. If you take out the gas pedal, or the tires, then the function of getting to my destination is severely affected.

Likewise, this principle applies to renewing your mind. Your mind is your mind. Your thoughts are your thoughts. The mistake which you saw that I made earlier, when trying to renew my mind, was that I assumed that all I needed to do was renew my thoughts. I see many sermons preached about renewing the mind, and in almost all of them, I see this exact misinterpretation occurring. For some reason, whenever we read this verse, we interpret it as saying, renew your thoughts. But the verse says to renew your mind; it doesn't say to renew your thoughts. This misconception about one's mind equaling one's thoughts has severely limited us. When I asked my friend for advice before, this is exactly what happened. I asked him how I could go about felling better, and his answer was that I needed to renew my mind. When I asked him, how do

I practically renew my mind, his response back to me was, whenever a certain thought comes to you, that says something that isn't true, then you need to replace it with a scripture that is true from the Bible.

How is it that as a body of Christ, we have read this scripture over and over again, and interpreted it as God wanting us to renew our thoughts? The scripture says be transformed by the renewing of your mind. It does not say be transformed by the renewing of your thoughts. It uses the word mind.

I decided to look up this word mind in the dictionary. Everyone, besides Christians, seems to know that one's mind is something greater than just one's thoughts. I don't know where this misinterpretation started, or for how long we have been misinterpreting the word mind, but it's time we start properly interpreting and understanding this scripture. Here is a definition for the word mind that I found: "the element, part, substance, or process that reasons, thinks, feels, wills, perceives, and judges, etc."[3]

Have we this whole time been incomplete in our understanding of what this verse is saying? I believe that if we are only trying to renew our thoughts, then yes we are. God wants us to be renewing our entire mind, and that looks like it includes a lot more than just our thoughts. It is not wrong to be renewing our thoughts; we will always need to do that. But we are definitely incomplete, if that is all we are doing. We are supposed to be renewing every facet of our mind, and that includes our desires, our will, our emotions, and our thoughts.

Not just our thoughts alone.

Trying to renew our mind by changing only our thoughts alone, will most likely lead to frustration and limited results. Going back to the car example from before, it needs oil, gas, and water to run properly. If you put in gas only, and forget to add the oil and water, then there is going to be a big problem down the road. Eventually if you keep adding only the gas, while forgetting to add the other two, then one day your engine will cease. At this point, the function of your car getting you places is no longer possible. Likewise, the same is true for renewing your mind. The function and purpose for renewing your mind is so that you can experience a transformed life. If you do not pay attention to all the things required for renewing your mind, then your results of a transformed life will suffer.

POSITIVE THINKING VS. RENEWING YOUR MIND

Renewing the thoughts you have inside of yourself will only be beneficial if you believe what you are saying. If you feel like a shameful, disgraceful, useless person with every fiber of your being, trying to replace those feelings inside with positive thoughts is not going to work. Even if you were to quote scriptures to go along with what you are declaring, your success is not guaranteed. The thoughts and scriptures need to be believed before they will have any success in working towards the goal of transformation that you are trying to achieve. Later on in the book, I will discuss what believing means, what it is not, and how we can practically do it.

I have seen so many people who feel negatively inside of themselves, and then try to fix the problem by creating positive thoughts. I feel this is the big myth, or stereotype, that people who don't fully understand the process of renewing your mind fall into.

Throughout this book, I may talk about positive thinking and renewing your mind interchangeably. Christians call the process renewing your mind, where as non Christians call this process positive thinking. The main difference that you see in positive thinking is that the individual tries to create what they are going to say to themselves. Whereas for renewing your mind, the biblical process of doing it, we look for scriptures to say over ourselves. It is my personal belief that using scriptures to speak over yourself is more powerful. It holds more weight to what is being said. It has a form of evidence built within it. That evidence being, God has said this, and I believe that God is not a liar, therefore what I am declaring over myself must be the true.

With that being said, many Christians still seem to fail at transforming their lives and fully renewing their mind. We will see later in the book the exact reason for this. It has to do with them trying to manufacture what God is saying about them by using their own voice to speak it over themselves, instead of having God speak it over them Himself. There is a major difference between these two things that you will continually see as a main theme as you read on. The difference will become clearer and clearer as you read through the chapters.

For now, I want to discuss in more detail the difference between positive thinking and renewing your mind. A non believer will still benefit from the process of positive thinking when they believe what they are saying to themselves. For example, if someone experienced a thought that said, "You are a bad person." They can quite easily say to themselves, right after they felt that thought, "I am a good person." If they believe that they are actually a good person, then they are going to experience success in feeling better.

In my eyes, a person who is a Christian will have an easier time believing this. The reason I say this is because they will be able to provide evidence as to why they are making this claim about what they are saying. In other words, they will be able to point to the required evidence that justifies why they are indeed a good person.

Let's take the same example above, where a person experiences a negative thought that says to them, "You are a bad person." This time a believer in Jesus may say, "I am a good person." They will add a scripture they know and say, "God is my creator, He loves me, He lives inside of me, and therefore I am a good person." Right away you can see that they have a bit more evidence and credibility for speaking against the negative thought that came.

The major difference between the two sets of belief systems will become even more evident as time goes on. Once the two people have spoken against the negative thought, most likely another negative thought is going to come back shortly after. This time it will have a questioning tone to it. A person may feel and hear something along the lines of an accusation.

Let's imagine the next negative thought that comes says, "You are not a good person. How can you say you are a good person? Don't you remember what you did last week? Remember how you got angry and swore at that person you were talking to. Then later you were totally judging that group of teenagers you walked by. How about that time you felt like stealing something in that store. How can you say you are a good person?"

I don't know if you can relate to the exact example I wrote above. If not, think of a situation unique to you, and replace the words I wrote with something you can remember. Most likely, whatever the details may be, the negative thoughts will have an accusatory tone to them. They often accuse an individual for something they did wrong. Other times the negative thoughts will try to accuse you of something you thought about, or felt. Either way, the goal of the negative thoughts is to make you feel guilty, to try and convince you that you are no good, and that you don't have any right to be claiming that you are good person.

I believe that this is the time where we can now start seeing the difference in belief systems that a person holds. To me a believer in Jesus knows that their identity isn't tied up in what they do. Their source of identity comes from Jesus Christ Himself. They may say, "I am not the sum total of what I do and what my actions say I do. I am free and forgiven of all actions that I do, and the truth of who I am is found in Jesus Christ. So since I believe that Jesus lived a perfect life and that He died to take my imperfection away in order to trade me His perfection, I am therefore perfect." So knowing this truth, and knowing who you are, will allow for an answer to be spoken back to the negative accusing thoughts we saw in the example before. You right away have an answer that disproves the last question the negative thoughts asked of you.

You see, the negative accusing thoughts will come to you and bring a bunch of evidence as to why what is being said must be true. Then at the very end an accusation will be made that implies, "With all this evidence against you, how can you claim to be good?" I always think of it like a court room battle going on inside of oneself, where there is evidence that speaks against you which points towards a guilty verdict. However, a Christian understands that Jesus Christ's verdict on the cross, of not guilty, supersedes all other evidence. That is why Jesus is the cornerstone of the Christian faith. It is why people look to what Jesus did by dying on the cross for all the answers that they need in life. This is why I believe a follower of Jesus has the ability to successfully replace negative thoughts with positive ones, and actually believe the new positive thoughts to be true.

Back to our example of a negative thought coming into your mind. A negative thought says, "Do you remember what you did last night. Do you know how bad that was? How can you say that you are a good person?"

A person who knows that their identity isn't based on what they do can respond quite easily. They could now respond with something along the lines of, "Oh I remember what I did. The good thing is that Jesus already forgave me over two thousand years ago when He died on the cross. Also, it is written in Romans 4:8, that *blessed is the one whose sin the Lord will never count against them*. Therefore, my God doesn't count what I did last night against me; He actually chooses to remember it no more. That is exactly why I can claim I am a good person. In fact, the next time I come across the same situation I experienced last night where I made that wrong decision, since I feel so wonderful now from finally understanding that God loves me unconditionally, and the fact that His opinion about me never changed when I made that wrong choice last night, now I will actually be enabled and empowered to make a better choice for myself in the future. So I won't actually be going down that road anymore. Thanks to my understanding of God's unconditional love, I will no longer be living that kind of lifestyle that I have been trying to get out of for so long."

With this kind of knowledge of what the Bible has to say, it is a lot easier to be able to replace negative thoughts with positive ones. In addition, the positive thoughts that you are replacing the negative ones with will now hold a lot more weight, and a lot more value. They become a lot more believable for an individual since God Himself has said it. Whereas, when someone tries to replace negative thoughts with positive thoughts on their own, they have to come up with the credibility of what they are saying on their own. Which I believe makes it quite a bit more difficult and problematic.

BAND-AID RENEWAL

We can see how a believer is going to have an easier time believing what they are saying about themselves. However, just because they are using these scriptures and speaking them aloud, it doesn't guarantee success. Even though what they are saying is the truth, it doesn't mean that it is true for them. What I mean by this is that just because they are saying truthful things that God has put in the Bible, it does not automatically become true for the person saying it; the person saying it still needs to believe that what they are saying is true. Without believing what they are saying to be true, then the transformation they desire will not occur.

This is what I meant earlier about the myth and stereotype that often comes along with renewing your mind. Just because a person keeps repeating something in their thoughts, and speaking it out loud with their mouth, doesn't automatically make it true. Someone could repeat something a thousand times to themselves, but it doesn't mean it will be true. You could keep saying a phrase and repeat it until the cows come home, but that doesn't automatically mean you will believe what you are saying. This same thing remains true, even when what you are repeating is scripture.

This myth I have seen over and over again when I listen to sermons that talk about the importance of renewing your mind. Although I have never heard a sermon where I disagree with what is being said regarding the importance of renewing your mind, I have yet to hear a sermon that fully explains the proper way to go about the process. This is exactly the area which stumped me for a while and hindered my breakthrough of a peaceful mind. Fortunately, God was able to reveal to me how to actually do it. That is, how I could go about practically renewing my mind so that I knew all of the steps that it required. Hence, this is exactly why I got motivated to write a book about it.

I mentioned earlier about the importance of fullness in a certain matter. Without the fullness of something, we miss out on a certain aspect. I used the example of a car, which needs gas, oil, and water, not just gas alone. Then I explained the definition of the word mind. How it includes more than just a person's thoughts. How it also includes a person's emotions and/or feelings, their will and/or desires, and their perception and/or memories. So a mind is made up of all of these different facets, each playing an integral part in its makeup. The mind is not just a person's thoughts alone.

To demonstrate the truth of this, I want to use a couple of real life analogies to drive home the point. Think back to an argument, or a disagreement, that you have had with a loved one. Think about how upset it made you. Or picture a situation that made you very angry, possibly with a coworker, or a good friend. So here you are right after it has all transpired, and your emotions are all over the place. Depending on the event you're thinking about, you may have been enthralled with anger, maybe you felt extremely betrayed, or possibly used. Whatever the emotion was for the event you are thinking about, it took away your peace momentarily.

For my illustration I am going to use the example of anger. Let's say I just got into a serious disagreement with my boyfriend/girlfriend and I am filled with anger. Now someone comes to me and tells me they have a solution for me. They tell me that I need to start thinking more positively. They tell me to start saying to myself the phrase, "I am not angry."

So I repeat that phrase a few times. "I am not angry. I am not angry… I am not angry."

Now they tell me I need to make it positive in tone. They mention, "Instead of saying I am not angry, try turning it into a positive sentence. Start saying to yourself, I am happy." Sound familiar? These are what positive affirmations are.

So I think to myself, "That seems more positive, I will give that a try." I decide to take the advice and I start saying to myself, "I am happy. I am happy. I am so happy right now. I love how happy I am right now… I am so happy." I keep repeating this all day long. I wake up the next day and say this phrase over and over again for the entire day.

Let me ask you a question. Do you think that I am eventually going to be happy by only using this repetitive technique of declaring positive words? The answer here is no. The answer may be a little unclear to you right now, but that's okay, I will come back to this example and explain it in more detail in the coming chapters.

This is the stereotype that I notice many people fall into when it comes to positive thinking, positive affirmations, and renewing their mind. People try to create words that mask what is truly going on inside of them. This is not going to work. A person will need both positive thoughts/words, and a way to deal with what is going on in the inside of them, in order to experience success.

I made this exact mistake in my own life and it never got me the result of transformation that I desired. It's like putting a Band-Aid over a bullet wound. Let's picture this example for a moment. A bullet was just shot into your skin. As a result, there is a big hole in your skin right where the bullet entered. There is also a bullet shell that is lodged and stuck inside of your skin. Not only that, but there is a fair amount of blood that is pouring out from the wound that was created. This seems like a major problem that needs definite attention as soon as possible. It would be insane to put a Band-Aid over top of it and expect the problem to be solved. First of all, the hole it caused in your skin can not be healed by a Band-Aid alone. You can put more and more Band-Aids on, keep replacing them every minute, but it is not going to do a thing for closing up the hole in your skin. A good solution would be to get stitches to close up the hole, then if you want to add a Band-Aid after the stitches are sewn, that would be a lot more effective. Secondly, there is a bullet lodged inside of your skin. I am not an expert on what bullet shells are made of, but I imagine it is not something that you want to leave inside of your body. The smartest thing to do would be to have a doctor take out the bullet shell from inside your skin. Furthermore, the best time to do this would be before the doctor puts stitches over the wound itself. With both of these things being done, the problem of excess bleeding would now be solved.

Imagine if you just tried to keep putting a Band-Aid over the wound. A bullet shell is inside of you, and there is a big hole in your skin right where it entered. Someone comes up to you and says, "That is a lot of blood that is pouring out of you, here is a Band-Aid to try and stop all of it." So you put on the Band-Aid. It quickly absorbs all of the blood pouring out, so you put another one on. The same thing happens again, so you put yet another one on. You repeat this a few times. Then the person giving the advice tells you, "Maybe you need more positive Band-Aids for this problem. Here are some bigger sized Band-Aids. They work a lot more positively." You decide to put one on. Over the course of the day, you keep putting on these more positive sized Band-Aids.

Now let me ask you another question similar to the one I just asked. Do you think that I am eventually going to be healed by only using this repetitive technique of using positive, big sized Band-Aids? Let me answer it along with you, no, I will not get healed! It's obvious to see the answer when I share an analogy such as this. The sad thing is that this is exactly what most people try to do when it comes to positive thinking, or renewing their mind. They think that by using their thoughts alone, and vocalizing aloud these thoughts through their mouth, that they will eventually solve the problem they are facing. I have done this exact thing myself, it does not work. Like I said before, you can't renew your mind by using your thoughts alone. You need to renew your entire mind which consists of many facets. These include your emotions/feelings, your will/desires, and your perception/memories.

Trying to renew your mind by renewing only your thoughts is what I call a Band-Aid solution. *We need to find the root of the problem, and not just fix what is on the outside only.* I believe much of what is done in our society today is people trying to fix problems only on the outside. We often over look the major causes in the first place. The very ones that are causing the problems that we are seeing. For example, if someone has difficulties sleeping at night, we are quick to prescribe a pill to fix the problem. I am not a doctor, so I am sure in some situations maybe that's what's needed to solve the problem. However, I am sure in a few cases people are not able to sleep at night because their thoughts are constantly going. Maybe they are constantly thinking about life, or maybe they are worrying about something they are going through. To me, in this situation, a pill may help them fall asleep faster, but it comes along with certain side effects. In addition, the constant reliance on a pill to fall asleep becomes problematic.

So on the outside, the problem of not being able to fall asleep gets fixed, but the problem a person has regarding worry and anxiety never gets fixed. The real root of the problem is that they have never learned how to manage worry and anxiety, and as a result it is affecting their ability to fall asleep. In other words, the trouble of sleeping is a byproduct of the constant worry, anxiety, and over-thinking. Instead of a pill for these people, they could just as easily be treated and taught how to manage thinking patterns, and how to deal with worry and anxiety. Psychologists and therapists often deal with people that have difficulties with these types of things. But we as a society are too quick to go for the Band-Aid solution as it seems easier and faster. Unfortunately, many times it causes new unforeseen problems down the road.

I feel this way of dealing with problems has crept into the church as well. Instead of wanting to deal with the root of the problems in our lives, we are often too quick to want a so called Band-Aid solution. The problem of doing that when it comes to our faith is that it is going to short-circuit the power. We are not going to reap the benefits that God wants us to have in our lives. When it comes to transformation in our lives, we need to do it God's way. The way that He told us to achieve this transformation was by renewing our minds. So if we believe what God says, then we are going to have to listen and do it His way if we expect to experience the blessings that He desires us to have. In this case, the blessing of a transformed life is achieved through the process of having your mind renewed. God did not tell us to renew our thoughts alone to obtain a transformed life. He told us to renew our minds in order to achieve this transformed life.

I don't know about you, but having a transformed life is something I assume we all want. I have yet to meet a single person who doesn't want at least one area of their life transformed. You name it: whether it is your peace, your relationships, your marriage, your finances, or your self-image, I am sure we all want something greater in at least one area of our lives. That is not the real question at hand, that one is usually a no-brainer. The real question is how do we practically renew our minds?

Like I said before, I have heard many sermons about the importance of renewing your mind. However, most of the ones that I have heard tell you to change only your thinking. I believe it is so much deeper than this. I believe we need to renew the entirety of our mind. In the next section of the book I will be describing in detail the major areas of the mind, and how to renew those areas. I believe that once a person's mind is fully renewed, they will experience the desired transformation God has promised. After learning about the practical steps needed to renew each part of your mind, I believe your life will never be the same again. By the end of the book I trust you will be able to see the importance of renewing each part of the mind, and I trust you will be able to achieve a transformed life, no matter who you are, and what you have gone through.

POWER *of* THOUGHTS

CHAPTER 3

Renewing the mind in the area of your thoughts is extremely important. Like I said earlier, this is the area that most Christians are familiar with and have the most practice doing. In this chapter, I will be exploring where thoughts are believed to come from. We all have thoughts; they are a part of our makeup, our DNA. Whether those thoughts that we experience are truthful, or beneficial to us, may be a different story. Recognizing how they are affecting our lives, and finding out where they stem from, is often a little bit more challenging. It takes reflection, and practice with observing certain thought patterns, to start realizing how important they really are. Whether you are familiar with renewing your thoughts, or this is the first time you have ever thought about the process, this chapter will help bring clarity and leave you confident about understanding the nature of thoughts.

It's hard to imagine someone overemphasizing the importance of thinking right. Right thinking is extremely vital in living the life we desire. Let's take two different people, with two different ways of thinking, to illustrate this point.

Someone who has limiting beliefs about themselves, and thinks in an extremely pessimistic and critical way, will not be able to achieve certain things. If you tell yourself every single day that you are no good, that you will never get a good job, and that you will never end up getting married, then that is what your life is going to be like. It is not possible for someone to tell themselves those three things day after day, for a period of time, and then one day magically wake up and find themselves living oppositely to what they have been saying.

Think about it, let's imagine I tell myself repetitively for 1000 straight days that I am no good, I will never get a good job, and I don't deserve to get married. As I go to bed on day 1000, about to wake up on day 1001, I am not going to find myself waking up and going to work at my wonderful job, while kissing my partner goodbye as I leave the house. It is physically impossible. If that is my only thought that goes into my brain for 1000 straight days, I am not going to experience a life contrary to what I have been saying. *It is impossible to achieve something you believe you can't do.* It reminds me of that saying that goes, if you think you can or you think you can't, you're right.

The only way for me to be able to wake up to a good job, and a spouse, would be to believe that I can find a good job, and that I can get married. It's a pretty basic principle. If I don't think at least one time during those 1000 days that I can get a good job, and can get married, then it will be impossible to achieve getting those two things. If at any moment in time during the 1000 days, I allow for the possibility of those things to occur in my life, then they become possible for me to walk into. But until I allow the thought of believing it is possible for those things to occur in my life, I can never experience them.

If this is to abstract for you, here is an analogy to explain what I mean. Imagine a door that has a lock on it. If you put in a key that is cut to the wrong size and try to unlock the door, nothing will happen. If someone hands you the right key, nothing will happen until you take the wrong key out of the door. There will be no room for the correct key to be put into the key hole while the incorrect key remains inserted. Only one key can fit inside the key hole at a time, it's impossible for two keys to be inserted at the same time. So if you wanted to open the door in this scenario, you would need to take out the wrong key before you could insert the correct key. Failure to do this would result in the door not opening. Likewise, the same thing goes with our beliefs. *It's impossible for us to hold contradicting beliefs*. You can't believe whole heartedly you will never get married, and then one day magically wake up married.

On the flip side, let's imagine a person who says and believes that they are a good person, that they can get a good job, and that they can get married. For this person it is possible for them to have the things they are saying come into their life. I don't know if I would make an absolute statement and say that they are guaranteed to have these things come into their life. There could be many more variables that could come into play that would determine whether or not this person experienced a good job and marriage. If this person truly wanted these things, believed they deserved them, and never doubted that they would come into their life, then I would say these things would be guaranteed to come. This again is my belief, and you are free to believe otherwise.

My point however is to focus on the first person who never believes something is possible. Not believing something is possible that you actually want to achieve in life, is problematic. It becomes a limiting belief. The limiting belief that I described in the first example is quite easy to see. It's fairly easy to see the limiting belief of a person who never believes they can achieve something. However, our thoughts and limiting beliefs are not always that easy to recognize.

I want to share an example of a limiting belief that is not so easily recognizable. I hear some of my friends say it, and have heard it spoken of as a stereotype, that we as a society seem to hold. That is, that marriage is often an end to something, rather than a beginning. I have heard many times people say that when you get married, your sex life will eventually end. Also, I have heard people say that when you get married, your freedom completely disappears, and you no longer have time to do anything for yourself. There is no doubt that this statement isn't completely true. It's a stereotype that some people have regarding marriage. In other words, it's a limiting belief that some people have regarding marriage.

Stereotypes are obviously dangerous because they take elements of things that are either true, or partially true, and they exaggerate it to be either true in all cases, or true in areas that aren't actually true. In the example regarding marriage, we see a couple of stereotypes. In any relationship or marriage, it is true that some of your freedom will disappear. Relationships consist of compromise, thus all the things that you once had time for when you were single, will now need to be prioritized. Some things need to be discussed with your partner, and you may need to compromise with them. Other times you may be able to keep doing whatever it is you are discussing, it all depends on the situation. However, it is not true that all of your free time will be gone. It would be very unhealthy to be in a relationship where you have zero free time to do the things that you love to do.

So one needs to be careful who they listen to, and what they are listening to, when it comes to another person telling them about married life. The same thing holds true as to who you should listen to about sex life inside of marriage. If you are not careful, you will start to entertain, which will move you closer to believing, the things that other people are saying and believing about marriage. It's always important to be careful and selective as to who you listen to, and who you take advice from. I don't think it's wise to be getting all your marriage advice from someone who just went through their fourth divorce.

The deceptive thing about limiting beliefs is they start out as subtitle stereotypes. No one getting married fully believes that their sex life will end and that they will have zero free time once they tie the knot. If they fully believed this, they would not be getting married in the first place. It may be a stereotype that they have heard other people talk about and they are hoping that it is not going to be true for them.

What happens to some people when they get married is they don't consciously renew their thinking. They keep the stereotype other people have said about marriage in the back burner of their thinking. When they perceive a situation come up in their marriage, which makes the stereotype they are holding seem truer, they begin to add more weight and truth to that stereotype they are keeping. Over the course of time, they experience more and more situations which make the stereotype seem more and more true. As time continues to go on, their belief about marriage continues to change until it resembles the stereotype they hold.

At the beginning of a marriage, both parties believe that they are going to be together forever. They believe that their love is different. They believe that what happened to other people they know will not happen to them. They believe that their sex life will remain strong, that they will have time for themselves, and time for the things that they love to do.

However, the ideas and beliefs that others around them hold regarding marriage may eventually creep in. Each experience that a person goes through can make the stereotype they are carrying look more and more true. If one does not carefully determine their own beliefs about marriage, they will be more susceptible to believing certain stereotypes and lies. Sadly for some, they go all the way down the path, and at the end of the road they end up fully believing in something that started off as a small and minor stereotype. In this example regarding marriage, the two people involved may decide to get a divorce. The destructive cycle will most likely continue, because when people ask them about what married life was like, they will answer according to what was true for them. In other words, what was true according to their experiences.

PERCEPTION

Just because someone perceives something to be true, does not automatically make what they perceive true. In this case, the people involved would perceive that marriage ruins relationships and love. People in our society perceive many things, but it doesn't mean all they perceive is true. It is true for them, but it doesn't automatically mean it is a universal truth. Someone who has fought in a war may perceive the world to be a dangerous place. But another individual could love traveling. They could have traveled to many countries and perceive that the world is a safe place. How could two people hold onto two different truths? The reason is because they are looking at it through a different lens. In other words, they hold different perspectives.

That brings up the question, what is the correct lens to have, and to look through? As Christians, the proper lens to look through would be to look at things through the word of God. That is, to look at things through what the Bible has to say about it. In the example before about marriage, if someone looked at it through the lens of the Bible, they would see what was true about marriage. They would recognize that what other people are saying about marriage is incorrect. They could take numerous examples from the Bible, and the people who are in it that were married, to find their answers. If they looked at Abraham's life, they would see right away that he and Sarah had a child late in life. Then one could easily conclude that they must have had sex together to produce that child, therefore sex life doesn't have to end because a married couple gets old. Nor is one's sex life over, or doomed, once marriage starts. Right away they have already disproved one of the stereotypes I mentioned. Then they could see that Abraham did many things for God in his life time, he was quite busy. Therefore, they could conclude that a person can still have free time to follow their dreams and passions inside of a marriage. Thus the other stereotype gets disproved, and lies about married life are exposed.

This is a good example of what renewing your thoughts looks like. In this particular example, the people involved were presented information, and a way of thinking, regarding what marriage is like. This type of thinking could have come from anywhere. It may have come from society, from friends, or from married people that they have observed during their life time. A person would be wise to ask themselves, is this information about marriage true? Is this how marriage has to be for everybody? These questions are very important in regards to marriage, and one should look to have these questions answered. In fact, I would say it is vital to the success of a marriage to have these questions answered. The answers to these questions are going to form the beliefs that an individual holds.

Maybe even more importantly then having these questions answered, is who is going to answer these questions for you? Will it be friends, society, popular opinion, a mentor, Gods word? Wherever the answer comes from, I would suggest making sure it lines up with God word. If it comes from a friend, or a mentor, are they getting their answer from God's word? For me, if advice or opinions on a matter doesn't come from God's word, and if it doesn't line up with what God has to say in the Bible, then I am going to disregard it. It reminds me of the words spoken in Romans 3:4, which say, *let God be true, and every human being a liar.*

When finding out answers to important questions about life, it is wise to look to what God says about the matter. As a society, we have never before in history been bombarded with so many choices. Even when it comes to choosing a cell phone, I can think of at least ten different brand names to choose from off the top of my head. I don't think we need to renew our mind and consult God as to which phone to go with. But we do face many other important choices in our life, such as who to marry, what career to choose, and what friends to have. If we don't renew our minds we will make the wrong choices for ourselves, and these decisions will lead us down roads that we don't desire going down.

Part of renewing our mind is renewing our thoughts. By renewing our thoughts, along with renewing the other parts of our mind, we become equipped, and enabled, to make the right decisions for ourselves in our life. Thus we end up traveling down roads that bring satisfaction, joy, and fulfillment, as we proceed walking through life's journey.

IMPORTANCE OF BALANCE

In the section before, we saw what can happen to people who start thinking and perceiving a certain way. Often times it starts out by partially believing a stereotype that somebody else holds to be true. It is at this point in time that we want to settle the issue of what is true in our thinking. If something is not the truth, and is contrary to the Bible, we want to recognize it as soon as possible, and change the thought to be true. We don't want to be unsure about something and let it linger in our thinking. It is better to be absolutely sure about certain things. So how do we recognize the thoughts that we have been holding onto for any length of time, the thoughts which may not line up with God's word? In other words, how do we recognize the negative thoughts that are forming wrong beliefs within us?

There are many steps that can help a person realize the thoughts that are occurring inside of them. The first one that comes to mind is to become aware of the thoughts occurring inside of you. If you notice that you quite often over-analyze and over-think, worrying about a negative thought for a long period of time before you recognize what you are actually doing, then becoming more aware of your thoughts is going to be beneficial.

I believe the way we become more aware of the negative thoughts inside of us is by being honest with ourselves. If you are having negative thoughts, it is best to become aware of them and look for a solution. Obviously ignoring them completely would not be a wise decision. Sweeping them under the rug is only going to create more problems down the road. But what is the best solution for dealing with negative thoughts? Many people believe focusing on positive things, or replacing the negative thoughts with positive thoughts, is the answer. If you ask me, I believe this statement and solution is only partially true.

Like I have been saying all along, partiality is not fullness. When something isn't full it means something is missing, and in this case, I believe the part that is missing becomes extremely problematic. It becomes a Band-Aid solution. Focusing on positive things is a good thing most of the time. However, when there is a problem, focusing on positive things can lead to someone completely ignoring the actual problem. Depending on the situation, actually focusing on the negative thoughts can be beneficial. What I mean by this statement is that focusing on the negative thoughts, and asking yourself the question why are they occurring, is sometimes the most important thing that we can do.

At certain times in life, counting your blessings, and thinking about positive things, is exactly what a person needs to do. But in life, a person also needs to understand balance. This solution will only work some of the time. Other times, focusing on the positive can be the worst thing for us. It can lead us down a path of ignorance and result in us being blinded to the actual root of the problem. Sometimes being comfortable with the status quo can be the worst thing for us, as it can keep us from ever reaching a higher potential.

Just like in the example of the bullet wound I mentioned last chapter, a healthy balance is needed to find the best solution, and course of action, in regards to fixing the problem. Let's imagine you just got shot in the arm, and someone comes to you and tells you to focus on the positive as your solution. They tell you that once you focus on the positive long enough, things will all work out and be fixed. That advice alone isn't going to cause the desired result of healing. If I were to take that solution and believe it as my only answer, I wouldn't receive the healing I needed. If I took it too far to the extreme, I would say something like, "Well at least I got my other arm. At least I got my two legs." This seems absolutely preposterous.

Can you imagine yourself having just been shot in the arm, and the only thing you do to try and move towards healing, is focusing on the positive. You say, "Well at least my other arm is still functioning. At least both my legs work."

Then all of a sudden, a thought comes into your mind that makes you aware of the pain that is stemming from the bullet wound. The thought says, "Your arm is no good, it is in pain. It's not going to be able to do anything in the future."

You hear the thought come up inside of your mind and you remember back to the solution that you heard works. So you tell yourself, "I need to think more positively and focus on the positive. This negative thought isn't going to defeat me. I know exactly what to do. I'm so thankful that my other arm works perfectly. I'm so thankful that both my legs are working. I am so blessed to have such a great functioning body."

You decide to repeat this phrase every time you hear the negative thought come to you and remind you that your arm is in pain. You think to yourself, "I'm so thankful I know what to do in this situation. I'm so glad I learned about positive thinking. Once I repeat this long enough to myself, everything is going to be okay."

If you aren't laughing hysterically to yourself already, or thinking what a crazy person; who in their right mind would do such a thing? Who would get shot in the arm and try to fix the problem by thinking positive things? That's absolutely ludicrous!

I agree. It is definitely quite obvious that this person is not going to have their arm healed using this technique. I am not a doctor, and don't know everything that a bullet wound can cause, but I imagine that one day either this person's arm will have to be amputated, or they will not live long enough to see that day because of the loss of blood that they will experience. Whatever the case may be, I think you get the point. When you're in pain, recognizing the pain, and being aware of it, is a major key. The solution of ignoring it completely, and focusing on positive things, is not going to do a thing. In fact, it will most likely make the situation worse.

As silly as this story seems, and as clear a principle this is to see, it is often exactly what we as Christians do when it comes to trying to renew our mind. Often times our mind is trying to bring our awareness to a problem. It is trying to bring our attention to a wound that we have inside of us, a wound that is slowly killing us from the inside, and a wound that is crying out for healing. But instead of recognizing and acknowledging the wound that bleeds deep within us, we end up ignoring it, thinking that it is a negative thought, or a spiritual attack.

I made exactly the same mistake when I first tried renewing my mind. I see my friends frequently falling into this deceptive trap as well. I also see the body of Christ as a whole, making this exact same mistake. I see a bunch of people, sitting in churches, wondering why transformation doesn't occur in their lives, especially when they try and start renewing their mind. I believe strongly that it is because we have misunderstood the exact practical process of how to fully renew the mind. We need to understand precisely how to renew our minds if we are ever going to experience transformation. We can't keep doing what we have been doing, never getting the desired results, and thinking all the while that we are on the right track.

I use the analogy of driving to a desired destination. If you think you are going down the right road and believe that it is a matter of time before you reach your destination, then you better be absolutely sure that you are on the correct road. If you came to a cross in the road and you were supposed to turn right, instead of going left, then you will be travelling farther and farther away from where you are trying to go. The faster you realize you have made a wrong turn, the quicker you can turn around and head towards the desired destination. The longer it takes you to realize it, the longer it will take to arrive at your destination. It's time we ask ourselves, are we going about renewing our minds in the correct way?

Like I was getting at before, many times we hear what we believe to be a negative thought and we turn to what we know best. We turn to positive thinking, and/or renewing our mind, or at least what we believe this process is supposed to look like. I have talked to so many people, listened to loads of sermons, and for some reason everyone seems to believe their mind equals their thoughts. Just the other day, I was talking to a friend of mine and he used the word mind while describing a story. As soon as I heard him say this word, I saw him point to his brain. I thought to myself, why didn't he point to his heart? Why didn't he point elsewhere on his body? Why do we think that the word mind always equates to our brain? Moreover, why do we think the word mind only equates to our thinking. It is so much deeper than that.

PROPER BALANCE BRINGS REST

So like I said, many times we hear in our thoughts what we believe to be negative thoughts, and we begin to start replacing them with positive ones; the more negative thoughts that come, the more we try and speak over them with positive ones. What results is a constant ongoing conflict within oneself. We hear a thought that is protective in nature, but label it as negative, and then we go about trying to speak over it. This ends up producing one of two results. It either produces a constant ongoing battle within the individual, where they feel like they are always at war within themselves, and as a result of this, they end up feeling the exact opposite feelings of peace. Or in the other case, the individual decides to give up on the arguing match going on inside of themselves, and they begin to look for ways to try and ignore the original thought all together. Often times this requires the person to look for things that will constantly keep them preoccupied with what they are feeling. Some people turn to drugs, sex, or alcohol to try and constantly keep themselves numb to feeling and hearing what is truly going on within them. Others may choose to keep busy through other outlets that are more smiled upon by society. These outlets could be anything, such as work, the gym, or a relationship. All these outlets have a common underlying motive: to keep oneself constantly busy so that they will never feel what is truly going on inside. In other words, whether the outlet is healthy or not, both solutions keep the individual just busy enough to numb the feelings and thoughts that would come if they decided to be completely still.

Jesus promised us that He would give us rest for our burdens. We see this in Mathew 11:28-30.

"Come to me, all you who are weary and burdened, and I will give you rest. Take my yoke upon you and learn from me, for I am gentle and humble in heart, and you will find rest for your souls. For my yoke is easy and my burden is light."
Mathew 11:28-30

For any individual who is weary and burdened, Jesus promises them the freedom to come to Him and receive rest for their souls. He makes this exchange absolutely free of charge. Satan will also give a person rest as well, but his rest will have a cost to it. His rest will be an imitation version of the true rest Jesus offers. Satan's rest will also only be a temporary fix.

I myself know what it is like to live a life of addiction. I remember two distinct times when I would need to turn to the addiction of my choice. The first was when I was overwhelmed with something in my life. The second scenario was when I went through something painful and traumatic. For individuals who feel overwhelmed with anxiety, loneliness, fear, etc...., an easy way to escape those feelings is by turning to something that will soothe them. If one goes out and drinks a lot of alcohol, they will momentarily forget about their issues.

For an individual who experiences a painful breakup, an easy way to not think about it, and to not feel the painful sting, is to go out and party at a night club, then when the night is over, try and find someone to go home with and continue actions that help suppress the feelings related to the breakup. It's not hard to see by looking at what is going on in our society today. You may have experienced friends who live this way, or you may have lived this way yourself. Even Hollywood depicts this solution through movies that are catered to the younger generation. I can think of hundreds of movies that have to do with people going through breakups, and what the characters do to resolve the issue. The message is simple: if you have gone through a breakup, go out and get wasted, find someone that is also looking for what you are looking for, and go home and have sex with them. If you are not familiar with this solution for dealing with a breakup, I would be very surprised. It doesn't take much to open your eyes and see what is going on. Sorry if I am being blunt with the truth, but I would rather mention what happens, then sweep it under the rug. There is nothing wrong with people who turn to that avenue to deal with a breakup, but shouldn't there be an alternative solution for those who may not want to choose that route.

You see, the enemy can bring an individual temporary relief to their problem. Getting drunk, or any other chosen outlet, will indeed provide relief for the individual's problem, but that relief will only be temporary and it will come at a cost. If this is your solution to the painful sting of a breakup, the pain will indeed go away for a while, but when the buzz of the alcohol wears off, you will find yourself right back to having the same problem. You can go about fixing that by deciding to go out and get drunk again the next night, but if you ask me, this seems like a solution that is not going to work out in the end. Not to mention, if one was to continue this solution for a long period of time, they are going to eventually feel the costly effects. I'm no expert on long term alcohol use, but I imagine that it has implications regarding cancer and liver failure.

There is a reason the Bible says that Jesus will give one rest from their burdens. It's because He knows that a person will not be able to successfully deal with them in any other way. I don't care who you are and how smart you are, you will not find a healthier and more successful way to get rid of your painful burdens than through Jesus Christ. Drugs, sex, porn, or alcohol; all of these things are not powerful enough to fix what a person feels inside.

I myself turned to a few of these things. When I experienced the pain of rejection that stemmed from a failed relationship, I wanted to jump into another one as soon as possible in order to not have to feel and deal with all the things that I was experiencing. Needless to say, this isn't the smartest motive to have when deciding to enter into a relationship. I thank Jesus that He showed me a better way to deal with such emotional hurt.

So in order to experience full transformation in our lives, we need to learn how to renew more than just our thoughts. In order to achieve a transformed life, we need to make sure the rest of our mind is healthy. If our emotions are hurting, no amount of renewing our thoughts will change the problem we hold in our emotions. We need to learn how to renew our emotions as well. In the next chapter I will continue to discuss the importance of renewing our emotions, as well as share how we can practically go about renewing them. With renewed thoughts, and renewed emotions, you will be well on your way to transforming your life.

POWER *of* EMOTIONS

CHAPTER 4

When it comes to transformation in our lives, we need to be accurate about the exact area we are trying to make positive. We don't want to experience negative emotions and make the error of perceiving them to be negative thoughts. If this mistake occurs, which I see happens quite often, I myself even fell into this trap, it will result in frustration and a life not fully transformed. One will end up just replacing the negative emotion with positive thoughts. When the negative emotion comes back and reminds you that it needs to be dealt with, you will keep trying to replace it with positive thoughts. This cycle will keep repeating and cause a great deal of frustration to the individual trying to change their life. It will start to take away the peace that person experiences and they will end up feeling like there is a constant battle going on within. Either the person will give up on the goal of trying to change their life, and just accept the situation they are in. Or they will continue to keep fighting the battle going on between their negative emotions and their positive thinking, hoping that if they can successfully stay positive in their thinking long enough, the things they are trying to improve and change will automatically get fixed over the course of time.

However, the truth and reality is that time will not fix this struggle. The individual who believes that this is what positive thinking is, or that this is what renewing their mind is, will be greatly disappointed in the end. They will never attain the desired transformation in the area of life that they are trying to achieve. If a person's emotions are fully functioning in a healthy and positive way, then replacing negative thoughts with positive ones will allow a person to attain the desired transformation they are trying to achieve. But this will only happen when their emotions are already in the correct state.

I don't want to use the word 'negative' to describe the state of someone's emotions. Their emotions are not a negative thing. Being hurt, being angry, or other similar emotions like these, are not negative emotions. It's okay to feel hurt, or to feel angry. It would actually be unhealthy to try and live a life where you are constantly trying to avoid ever feeling hurt or angry. But these emotions become negative to us if they are not released properly and effectively. So this is what I am meaning when I refer to 'positive' and 'negative' emotions;

positive if they are dealt with correctly, and negative if they are not properly handled.

If a person gets angry, or hurt, and they don't deal with it properly, over the course of time it will catch up with them again. Have you ever heard someone say you can't run away from your problems? That is because it is true, life will circle around, and the issue will catch up to you again and create more problems in the future. This is what I mean by 'negative' emotions. The state of someone like this has negative emotions because they do not deserve to be holding onto hurt, or anger, for that long of a period. A person in this negative emotional state will not experience healing through thinking positively, or through renewing their mind, if their solution only includes using their thoughts. In other words, it will be impossible for them to achieve transformation in certain areas of their life if they only focus on renewing their thoughts alone. A person can't change a negative emotional state by trying to create positive thoughts. If they feel a negative emotion surface from within them, they will not be able to replace it with a positive thought and expect to see results. They could try and continue this process every minute of their waking day for an entire year, but nothing will change.

The difference between the two examples is seen by looking at what is occurring in the emotional state of an individual. I want to explain three different cases that can occur in regards to positive thinking, or renewing of the mind, and explain the transformation success of each case.

Case 1. In a positive emotional state, a person who is switching negative thoughts to positive thoughts will experience success in their desired transformation.

Case 2. In a negative emotional state, a person who is switching negative THOUGHTS to positive thoughts will still actually experience success in regards to transformation. But the success will be limited as they will only be able to see transformation/changes to their lives in certain areas.

This is where I think the stereotype and misconception comes from regarding positive thinking, or renewing your mind. Since a person sees some results from the process they are doing, of switching negative thoughts to positive ones, they think that they will be able to do that exact same process all of the time and experience successful results. But that isn't true. What has even greater influence over the thoughts themselves is the emotional state.

Case 3. In a negative emotional state, a person who is switching negative EMOTIONS to positive thoughts will experience zero success in their desired transformation. This is because the negative emotion they are trying to change is not negative in nature. It is actually protective in nature, and the thought it produces inside of the person is actually trying to remind the person to deal with the preexisting problem. If the person ignores the protective thought, they will continue to struggle through life. Like I mentioned earlier, a person can ignore this problem in many different ways. People with addictions often turn to a substance to help them ignore the emotion. They know that if they can numb the emotion, the emotion will never have the chance to turn into a thought. If it never gets turned into a thought, they will never be able to hear the issue. Since the issue is never heard, the individual then starts trying to convince themselves that the problem is solved. That is why one of the first steps in a recovery program is for a person to acknowledge and admit that they do have a problem. It is clear to see that this ignorance will not solve the problem. Trying to change a negative emotion by speaking overtop of it, with a contradictory positive thought, tries to accomplish this exact same thing. It ends up becoming another outlet a person uses to try and ignore the protective thought.

The obvious goal for any person in this case is trying to get rid of the negative emotional state that they are experiencing. Many people believe that speaking positive thoughts will eventually turn their negative emotional state around. They are hoping the positive thoughts will completely silence the thoughts and feelings they experience coming from their negative emotional state. This is exactly why it doesn't end up working. If someone actually possessed the power and ability to do this, what they would be able to accomplish would actually be harmful to them in the end. Since the thoughts and emotions are protective in nature, if people could actually succeed in getting rid of them through positive thoughts, it would mean that people had the ability to self destruct themselves. If that were true, then people who experience high levels of pain in their life would then be in jeopardy of the possibility of self destruction. This ability would be counterproductive for human nature and the goal of preservation. Thus, it is impossible to do this. Which in turn means it is impossible for someone to expect transformation, or change, solely based on positive thoughts alone. There is a set law in nature about self protection that is physically impossible to get around.

Remember the example before that I shared about the bullet wound. It can't be fixed solely on positivity, or positive thinking. There needs to be some course of action with regards to the wound. Likewise, in this case, there needs to be some course of action taken towards changing the negative emotional state. Moreover, the action must take place on that exact specific level, not on a level that holds less weight or power. This is exactly why I believe that a person who is in a negative emotional state, and decides as a solution that they are going to solely switch negative emotions to positive thoughts, will experience zero success in their desired transformation. The solution will come when they change their negative emotional state to a positive emotional state. Then they will be able to experience what a person in Case 1 can experience, which is, they will be able to successfully take negative thoughts and make them positive. They will be able to transform their life.

We all want to have the power to be able to transform our lives. We all possess the ability to achieve this within ourselves. It's not a question of whether or not we are capable. Many of you may have tried to change your life before, but when you tried you felt like nothing happened. I myself went through the same frustration. I never was able to experience any success in regards to transforming my life until I understood the differences between these 3 cases.

NEGATIVE THOUGHTS VS. NEGATIVE EMOTIONS

So how do we know what case we fall into? I want to share what I remember experiencing, and how I was able to tell what case I fell into. Another option is to ask Jesus to make it clear to you what case you fall into. Awareness as to what case you fall into will be the key to your starting point. Earlier this year I found myself trying to explain something to my friend, and I wrote him a text message to try and portray my point to him. I want to share the text here, as I feel it is a good analogy of what I mean when I say that awareness is a major key that needs to be understood before anything can actually happen.

Here is the text that I wrote him:

Imagine for a second that you were a glass and I was a jug of water. Let's say that being full of water was the goal that you desired and wanted. If you were empty and I came to you and said, "I want to fill you up with water." If you are completely empty, but in your mind you think you're full, you will say to me, "I am already full of water; I don't need any of your water to fill me up." I will go away, and you will be left believing you are full of water, but in actuality you will remain empty. But if you were empty and I came to you and said, "I want to fill you up with water." If you were to say, "Ok, go ahead, I am empty," I will fill you up, leave, and after I am gone away, you will be left filled up.

Then I asked my friend what is the moral of the story? What I was trying to explain to him was that if you believe everything is okay, but it is actually not, then you are not going to take any action to fix anything because you don't even think there is a problem. But the minute you become aware that there is a problem, you can then start looking for a solution. No one will look for a solution to a problem if they don't believe that a problem exists. Likewise, in the 3 cases above, it is extremely vital to be able to recognize there is a problem. After you come to this realization, you can start looking for the right solution. In cases 1 and 2, a person must recognize the negative thought first before they will know that they should replace it with a positive thought.

Like I mentioned earlier, it becomes extremely problematic for our lives if we think we are in case 2, but in actuality we are in case 3. In other words, if we believe we are replacing negative thoughts with positive thoughts, but in actuality we are trying to replace negative emotions with positive thoughts. If this occurs, we will never begin to look for a different solution. So it's vital we become aware of the difference between a negative thought and a negative emotion. So how do we distinguish between the two? You can ask Jesus to show you if something is a negative thought or a negative emotion. I believe that will work. Another way to tell the difference is to see how frequently it occurs. This is how I was able to tell the difference. This is how I distinguish between a negative thought and a negative emotion.

I don't think any person will ever be completely free from having the odd negative thought come into their thinking. I have heard many people use this popular phrase which goes, "You can't stop the birds from flying over your head, but you can prevent them from building a nest in your hair." What is meant by this phrase is that it is impossible to stop negative thoughts from coming into your thinking from time to time. But you can prevent the negative thoughts from building into something bigger inside of you, by taking action. So if you experience negative thoughts once in a while, then most likely they are only negative thoughts. If you replace them with positive thoughts and they don't seem to come back to you, then most likely you concluded correctly that it was a negative thought.

If the negative thoughts seem to come to you very frequently, and after you replace them with positive thoughts they seem to never go away, they just come back even stronger and with even more frequency, then most likely they are more than negative thoughts. In this case, it is highly likely that they are actually negative emotions. They are emotions that are not in a healthy state that want to be released, and they are manifesting themselves as protective thoughts. But most people misinterpret these types of thoughts and conclude that they must be negative thoughts, when in actuality they are protective in nature. They are stemming from an emotional state that was caused by a negative experience that the person went through. The protective thoughts are occurring to remind the person that the experience needs to be fully healed from. Until the experience is fully healed from, the individual won't be able to walk into the life that they dream of since their past hurt will cause fear. This fear keeps the person paralyzed from moving towards their dreams. So the protective thought is actually trying to help the person heal from that experience, so they can move forward and live life to the fullest.

However, what most people try to do is replace the protective thought, which is stemming from a negative emotion, with a positive thought. They think that if they just repeat positive thoughts long enough, then they will walk into that. They believe that they will just manifest what they keep repeating.

Let's take someone who lives in a negative emotional state. They dream about getting married in the future. They decide to repeat to themselves positive thoughts that sound something like this, "I deserve to find an amazing spouse. I am an amazing person, I will be married soon. I have so much to offer in a relationship. I have so much love to give, and I deserve so much love in return." These things are all true, the person does deserve all of these things, and they do have the capability to give and receive all that love. But they are going to have a really hard time believing that this is true, even if they were to repeat this set of positive thoughts several times throughout the day for an entire year. The reason is because the hurtful experience that they have not fully gotten over will speak louder than the words they speak out of their mouth.

A person's negative emotional state holds a lot more weight and value compared to all the words that same person can rehearse in their thoughts, or speak out of their mouth. If there is a disconnection between these two, nothing will happen. Once a person is able to change their negative emotional state to line up with what they have been saying, they will experience believing what they have been saying all along, and this will happen instantaneously. It is impossible for someone to change what is true in their negative emotional state through constant repetition of thoughts and/or words alone. Even if the words they are speaking and declaring are taken from scripture verses for more validity. What you say, no matter how many times you say it, will not change the way you feel inside of your negative emotional state. But the minute you change/renew your negative emotional state to a positive emotional state, you will believe automatically what you had been trying to believe with what you had been saying. This might be a little bit confusing right now, but later on when I share a few examples, you will know what I mean.

This is the mistake I see from people who practice positive thinking, or renewing the mind, make over and over again. They fall into this trap of trying to change their negative emotional state with the power of positive thinking. It will not work! I myself fell into this trap and experienced zero success. Like I said before, the reason it will not work is because the thoughts are stemming from a negative emotional state. The root of the problem is found at the level within the emotional state. The problem is not arising on the level of the thoughts. It's a Band-Aid solution to try to fix and repair the emotional state with positive thoughts. Just like the example of the person trying to fix the bullet wound with positive thinking. Many of us hold this exact same misconception about what renewing the mind actually looks like. Like I said, even I fell into this exact trap and misconception. Thankfully, I have the personality to not stick with things that don't give me results. So after trying this process for a few days, I gave up and looked for a better solution. Shortly after, I discovered where the actual problem lay, and I went looking for a solution to the new problem that I saw.

To illustrate this point even further, I will discuss exactly what happened to me during my journey of renewing my mind in the next section. I trust that after reading what happened to me, you will be able to see and recognize the difference between a negative thought and a negative emotion. Then once you understand the difference, you will be able to apply the practical steps that I will discuss later in the book. You will then be equipped to achieve the transformed life that you have longed for, and that the Bible promises to those who fully renew their minds.

PERSONAL LESSONS FROM RENEWING MY MIND

I started sharing what I went through earlier in chapter 2. I mentioned I went through a difficult period in my life where I heard some news that really hurt me. I fell back into an old way of life that I thought I had fully gotten over. I got so frustrated and didn't know what to do. I called my friend, and he gave me the advice of renewing my mind.

So I asked him, "How do I do that? How do I renew my mind?"

He responded back by saying, "Whenever a certain thought comes to you and says something that isn't true, then you replace it with a scripture that is true from the Bible."

This was great advice and would have fully worked if my emotional state was positive. My emotional state was anything but positive, as I soon discovered. His advice, which I see so many people try to use in their own lives, and it's what they will teach other people to do, will only work if you are already in case 1. That is, if you have a positive emotional state to begin with. But if you are already in a negative emotional state, then that advice alone will not work.

Where people make the mistake and misconception is when they take the word 'mind' from scripture, and they conceptualize it to mean only thoughts. However, that is only part of what the mind is. It is an incomplete definition. Thus, the results of a transformed life will be conditional. If only the thoughts of a person need renewing, and all the other parts of their mind are healthy, then successful transformation will take place. But transformation will only be effective under these set conditions. Change any of the conditions, without changing the process, then transformation will not occur because the process no longer fits the problem at hand.

The truth of this is easy to see by looking at another key analogy. Imagine you live out the process of coming home, looking under the mat, grabbing a key under the mat, putting the key in the door, turning the key, then finally opening the door and walking inside. If you change just one variable here, the process will no longer work. Let's say someone changes the key under the mat and everything else remains the same. So you come home, look under the mat, grab the key, put it in the door, turn the key, but this time you aren't able to open the door and get inside. Why not? Because a condition or variable has changed, which means the process before won't work here in this situation. The process of changing negative thoughts to positive thoughts will work when the emotional state is positive. Change the emotional state to negative, and you will need a new process. So since my emotional state was unhealthy, or 'negative,' the process I was told to follow never had a chance to succeed, which I found out shortly after.

So back to what was truly going on as I was trying this limited process of renewing my thoughts.

Negative Emotion: "You're no good. You're a terrible person. You're never going to amount to anything in this world."

Myself (Positive Thought): "I am a great person. I am going to do amazing things in this world. I was created for greatness."

I tried doing this on and off for two or three hours. That is, every time I felt the negative emotion speak the phrase above to me, I would speak against it with this exact positive thinking phrase above. After a few hours, I decided to ramp it up another notch and start using scripture. Here is what it looked like.

Negative Emotion: "You're no good. You're a terrible person. You're never going to amount to anything in this world."

Myself (Positive Thought): "I am a great person. God makes me great. The Bible says Jesus died for me, and that He loves me. I'm going to do amazing things in this world. I can do all things through Christ Jesus who strengthens me. I was created for greatness. God is my Father and He created me. He created me with a purpose. He created me for greatness. His thoughts about me are more numerous than all the sand on the seashores. He knows the exact number of hairs on my head. He knows how great I am, and about all the good things that are in store for me in my life."

Over the course of two days I repeated this process quite frequently. I would hear the negative emotion say something very similar to what it did above. After I heard the negative emotion, I would again say a positive thought similar to what I said above, but this time I had scripture involved. I was very motivated to keep repeating positive thoughts every time I heard a negative emotion.

Once I got ready to go to sleep the second day, I was completely exhausted from this constant conversation going on inside of myself. I remember saying to myself, "This is absolutely pointless. I feel like I am in a constant argument with myself. This is exhausting. I don't think this is working. What am I missing?"

After giving up and finally seeing that this process was not working, I got a new thought. I remember thinking to myself, "When I was born, the day I came out of my mother's womb, I wonder if I had all these negative thoughts going on inside." I obviously can't remember that day, but I concluded that I wouldn't have had the frequency of these negative thoughts coming to me on that day. After this made sense, I then thought to myself, "If these thoughts were not bombarding me on the day I got born, then they must have started from somewhere. Let me try to figure out exactly where and when they started, and then fix that. Why am I trying to fix them by speaking over them, when I could be trying to find out where they originated. Why don't I do that first, and then try to fix the problem there."

As soon as I had thought this, it seemed a lot more logical to me than what I was doing. I figured, "There must be a root issue somewhere that is causing all these negative thoughts to come to me in the first place. Let me fix the root issue, and once I am able to do that, I don't think the negative thoughts are going to come to me with such frequency any longer. All I am doing by speaking over top of them is just ignoring the root issue of why they are occurring in the first place."

I didn't know what I was actually doing at the time, but after living it out and looking back on it, I can clearly see what the problem was, and why I was experiencing so many negative thoughts. There was a root issue inside of me that was trying to cry out and get my attention, so that I could recognize that there was a wound inside of me. These thoughts were not negative at all. I heard them negatively because they sounded negative, and they felt negative. But the reason I perceived them as negative was because I had been ignoring a painful wound. How was I ever to know that I needed to ask for healing, if I never was aware that there was a wound? These thoughts were trying to bring my attention to a wound. They were actually not thoughts at all, they were feelings. They were the feelings I felt about myself. They were what I believed about myself.

What they were saying was what I was actually saying and believing about myself. I believed I was no good. I believed I was a terrible person. I believed I was never going to amount to anything in this world. I was trying to use positive thoughts, and true scriptures, to try and change what I believed about myself. I found out that if you believe within yourself, in your emotional state, that you are no good, then that is not going to change by telling yourself in your thoughts, and through the words out of your mouth, that you are indeed good; even if you state a scripture that declares that you are good in your thoughts, and then repeat it out of your mouth. Nothing will actually change. No transformation will occur in your life. The reason for this is because you won't actually believe what you are saying. In regards to my experience, my emotional state needed to believe that I was indeed good. I needed to renew my emotional state to believe that. In other words, I needed to renew my full mind, and not just my thoughts.

IMPORTANCE OF RENEWED EMOTIONS

We spend so much time learning about how to change our thoughts from negative to positive, but we never spend any time focusing on learning how to change our emotional state from negative to positive.

The scripture in Romans 12:2 states: *be transformed by the renewing of your MIND.*

This scripture does not say: *be transformed by the renewing of your THOUGHTS.*

If you were to amplify this scripture it would read: *be transformed by the renewing of your mind (your thoughts, your will, your emotions, your perceptions, your memory, etc.)*

In the exact same way a person needs to renew their thinking, they are going to have to renew their emotions. This renewing of the emotions is the part that I learned about. This is what I wasn't doing when I tried to renew my mind. I was only focused on renewing my thoughts alone. This is exactly why I didn't see the success that I wanted. It's exactly why I was never able to transform my life and get the peace that I wanted after I heard about the news that I received. I wasn't properly exercising what this scripture was telling me to do. I was missing out on the fullness of the scripture. I was missing out on the fullness of the definition regarding the word mind. As a result, I was using a process that wasn't the right one. The process I was using was never going to enable me to achieve my desired results. That is why I spent chapter 1 explaining the importance of fullness, so that you would see and understand what can be robbed from one's life if fullness is not comprehended and understood.

If you have tried using this scripture before, and have spent time renewing your mind, you should be able to recognize right away whether or not it worked for you. If it has not worked for you, it is not because God's word is incorrect. God's word is powerful and it always works. What is more likely the reason that transformation didn't occur for you is because you were making the same mistake that I made. If you haven't experienced the fullness of a transformed life, then most likely you have been reading this scripture and thinking it was telling you to renew your thoughts alone. Once you understand that it is telling you to renew the entirety of your mind, you will begin to redefine the process you are using. You must understand that renewing your emotions is just as vital as renewing your thoughts are.

If you fail to recognize this truth, you will continue to use a process that will not work. You will be left doing what you have always done, hoping that if you can just keep doing it long enough, that success will come. A person can turn the key over in a car that has no engine in it, and no matter how long they do it for, and no matter how much they believe that the car will start one day, it won't change the fact that the car will never start.

So how do we actually renew our emotions? What do we practically have to do? What are the practical steps? I will discuss what I learned to practically do in the coming chapters. The process of renewing our emotions is similar to renewing our thoughts. When one renews their thoughts, they take thoughts that are not true and replace them with thoughts that are true. In other words, the untrue thoughts are negative and we begin replacing them with true thoughts that are positive. This process of transferring one thing for another will be exactly what we use to renew our emotions.

So where do we go to find out what is true? We go to the word of God. More specifically, we look to Jesus. Jesus said of Himself in John 14:6:

Jesus answered, "I am the way and the truth and the life..."
John 14:6

We also read in John 1:17 *...grace and truth came through Jesus Christ.*

So how do we know what is true? We look at Jesus. Truth is a person and His name is Jesus. This is exactly what we are doing when we renew our thoughts. We are taking any thought that is out there, especially the ones we perceive, and making sure it lines up with the Bible. If it does not, then we cast it down and replace it with what is true.

Likewise, we need to do the same thing with our emotions. We need to take all of our emotions and look towards Jesus. Any emotion, or feeling, that isn't true, we replace it with a true emotion. It is the same idea of what you do with your thoughts. This will be more difficult to understand in regards to what to practically do, since many of us have never learned how to do it before. We have had lots of practice replacing our thoughts for Jesus' thoughts. But we don't have as much practice replacing our emotions with Jesus' emotions. But just like anything else, the more you practice doing it, the better you will become at being able to do it. In the next section, I will discuss how one's emotional state becomes negative in the first place. I will also discuss what occurs when the emotional state remains negative. After we understand the effects of a negative emotional state in our lives, we will understand the importance of renewing it, and getting ourselves back into a positive emotional state. After we understand all of this, no part of us will want to remain in that negative emotional state. Then we can finally learn what we have to practically do to get ourselves back into a positive emotional state. Once we practically learn how to get back to that positive state, we will start to effortlessly experience the benefits of a transformed life. After all of this, we will never read the Bible the same way again. We will read scriptures like we see in Psalm 37:4:

Take delight in the LORD, and he will give you the desires of your heart.
Psalm 37:4

We will know exactly how to take delight in the Lord, and one day we will look at our life and say, I have all the desires of my heart.

CAUSES OF A NEGATIVE EMOTIONAL STATE

We are beginning to see the importance of being in a positive emotional state. In a positive emotional state we have the ability to transform every area of our lives. What is more challenging for people is either entering into a positive emotional state, or remaining in one. I personally don't believe someone can get into this positive emotional state without loving themselves. I also don't know how a person is going to love themselves unconditionally without knowing Jesus. You're totally free to disagree with me on this belief, but I don't know any other way one can change their emotional state without Jesus as their source.

I want to share more about what I mean by a negative emotional state. I will start by explaining how a person gets into a negative emotional state in the first place. Then I will discuss what I believe happens to person who remains in that state. By the end of the book, I trust you will know what you can practically do in order to get out of the cycle of a negative emotional state.

A person will enter into a negative emotional state from anything that they experience in life that is extremely hurtful, painful, or traumatic. Anything that causes us to feel emotional pain is going to create hurtful emotions inside of us. There are many experiences in life that can cause a person to feel high levels pain or trauma. I won't mention every single scenario a person can go through, if I did, I don't think I would ever be able to finish this book. On top of that, every person experiences pain a little bit differently, and every painful situation someone goes through will also differ. How someone deals and copes with their pain is going to differ from person to person as well. For the sake of understanding, I will generalize a few examples to demonstrate what happens to a person who goes through a painful and/or traumatic experience.

Divorce is a great example of an experience that is going to cause trauma to the people involved. It seems like more and more divorces are occurring in our society today. I don't know if we fully understand how devastating the effects of this experience are on all the people involved. First of all, you have the two people getting the divorce in the first place. At some point in time they were deeply in love, and they decided they wanted to spend the rest of their lives together. This is a big commitment and vow to take with each other. Going from a period in time of being deeply in love, to a period in time where one is getting divorced, is quite a change in extremes. There is no question that this is going to cause emotional damage. Not to mention all the emotional hurt that the couple already experienced in their marriage before the actual day of the divorce. Often times there are also children involved. The divorce is going to cause emotional hurt to each child that exists in the family. These emotional hurts will cause deep wounds inside of each person connected to the event. There may even be extended family that feels the effects of the painful experience. I have no idea how far reaching this hurtful experience of divorce can go. Whatever the case may be, there is no question that the experience will cause hurt. Each person involved will experience the hurt in their own unique way, and each person will look to try and relieve that pain in their own unique way.

I never experienced a divorce in my life, so I can't fully relate to anyone who has experienced that kind of event in their lives. To tell people that I understand what they are going through would not be helpful in my opinion. First of all, I haven't gone through that type of experience, so it would be impossible to be able to fully understand the effects that they are experiencing. Second of all, I am not them. Every person has a unique way of seeing things, feeling things, and experiencing things, so even if I experienced a divorce in my family, other people's experience of divorce would not be identical to my experience. The only generalization we can really make about the experience of divorce is that it is going to cause emotional pain. As a result, a person is going to get into a 'negative' emotional state.

So we see that a painful experience is going to cause a person to enter into a negative emotional state. The pain can enter through any number of hurtful experiences, such as divorce, rape, abuse, or abandonment; the list goes on and on. Even a break up between two people who aren't married can cause a person to enter into a negative emotional state.

Technically it is not a divorce, since the two people are not married, but there is no denying the fact that there will be painful wounds and scars left over. I could list and categorize painful experiences all day. I suggest that you as the reader personalize your experience as you read through the rest of the book. Whatever the situation is that you went through, I recommend you compare it with the generalizations I make.

For myself, I never handled breakups that well. Every girl that I dated in my past, I turned to unhealthy outlets to relieve the pain. Needless to say those outlets never worked. I ended up creating even more problems for myself in the future. I feel that I'm not alone in the fact that I had no idea what to actually do after a breakup. I'm guessing a lot of you still have no idea what to do. I see so many people today who have no idea what to practically do when they go through a painful breakup. If you ask people on the street, you will get a whole bunch of different answers. Some people's solution is to go out and party, have fun, get drunk, and enjoy being single. Other people may tell you to find a new partner, and that will help you get over the pain. Other people may even tell you to give up on dating, just sleep around and have sex with people, that way you don't have any responsibilities. Their thinking is that you will get all the benefits of being in a relationship, without the risk of the pain that can come if you breakup. Since you are never fully committed to someone, it can't be painful if it doesn't work out, since you never committed in the first place. I don't know about you, but I don't want to be taking my advice regarding relationships from society, or based on public opinion.

All these solutions that you could possibly hear from people have one thing in common. They all try and deal with a hurtful experience through certain outlets. Each solution is counting on the fact that the pain will go away on its own. The thinking is, if you break up with someone just go ahead and find a new partner, over the course of time the pain will go away on its own. Just even writing it I can see the fallacy of the statement. But as ludicrous as it sounds when I write it, and as silly as it sounds when you read it, we either all have done it, or we see people who continue to do it, all the while thinking that it will work for them. Either we are blinded to the fact that these types of solutions won't work out, or we have become accustomed as a society of not knowing what to truly do, that we just don't care anymore. We just try to get by in life doing the best we can.

Honestly, when is the last time you remember someone teaching you how to deal with pain? I think it would be hilarious to show up at a doctor's office and say, "I have a broken heart. I just went through a break up with a girlfriend. I am really hurting and in a lot of pain." I wonder what the doctor would prescribe. It always blows my mind that we have cell phones, the internet, satellite TV, and other scientific advancements, but we don't have a solution for a broken heart. If we don't practically know what to do when we go through a breakup, how can we overcome experiences of divorce, abuse, or abandonment?

What occurs after hurtful experiences is a wound that bleeds deep within a person. This wound resides at the very core level of their being. This core level is what I refer to as the emotional state. After experiencing a painful situation, an individual will experience a bleeding so to speak, within their core emotional state. This bleeding will continue until something is done to fix it. A solution with the right course of action will be the only thing that can truly stop this so called inner bleeding. Using positive thoughts, saying positive things, or repeating truthful scriptures to try and stop this inner bleeding, will not work.

This wound that forms from a hurtful experience will take on a life of its own inside of the person. A new voice will begin to develop within the individual. Another way to put this is as soon as someone goes through a painful experience a voice will be birthed within them. This voice will remind the person of that painful experience. The voice will sometimes manifest itself as thoughts that can be heard by the individual. Other times it will manifest as a feeling, a frequency, or a vibration. It is this voice that is impossible for us to silence by either trying to speak over it, or trying to ignore it.

When one is still and quiet for long enough, they can actually hear what is going on inside of themselves. When a person does this, they can then perceive and hear this voice manifesting in the form of thoughts. This is why many people who are hurt and wounded try and occupy their time by staying busy. Their goal in keeping busy is to keep their focus and attention off of the pain and hurt going on inside of them. This act of keeping busy numbs and silences what is truly going on deep within them. Some people use drugs, sex, or alcohol in order to silence their inner pains. Some people overwork themselves so they never have the time in their day to feel their inner pain. Some people try to fill their days with as many things that make them feel happy, so that the feelings of happiness will outweigh the feelings of inner pain. They may choose to workout, go shopping, or always be around friends. The hope behind this is that the increase in happiness will work towards silencing and numbing the inner pain.

But no matter if a person tries to ignore the pain within, or face it head on, the fact that it remains inside of them will remain true. The difference will come in how the pain tries to get the individuals attention, because remember after all, pain will not automatically go away. It will always try to get a person's attention, and this is not a negative thing. It is trying to be heard for the purpose of healing and release. It's a natural law for pain to be felt. If it didn't work that way, then a person could have a cut on their neck or back, somewhere they could not see, and possess the possibility of bleeding to death while never becoming aware of it. So pain holds a purpose in our overall health and well being. Pain is not necessarily a negative thing.

The same thing applies with emotional pain and emotional wounds. Its purpose is to be heard so that we can draw our attention to that area and know that there is a problem that needs fixing. So if a person tries to preoccupy themselves with whatever outlet they choose to use, and never hear the pain speak to them, the pain will do whatever is necessary to speak and relay its message so that it's heard. This will come in the form of feelings, emotions, frequencies, or vibrations. If the person doesn't preoccupy themselves, then the pain can speak more directly to that individual, and often times be heard in actual words through that person's thoughts. Either way, it is impossible to ignore pain and run away from it. Have you ever heard the saying, you can't run away from your problems. There is a reason that saying exists.

What I see so many people try and do with positive thinking, or renewing their mind, is they will perceive a negative voice inside of themselves, and they will then try to speak over it with positive words, or with truthful scriptures. If the person's perception and conclusion is wrong regarding whether they are hearing a negative thought or a negative emotion, then a major problem arises. Like I said earlier, if it's a negative thought and you replace it with a positive thought, everything will be okay. But if it's a negative emotion and you try to replace it with a positive thought, then a real danger arises. That danger being a person using a process that they believe will work, but in actuality it will never work. What they will be doing is trying to speak over a voice that they can't successfully speak over. The reason is because it is impossible to speak over a painful voice with positive thinking, or constant repetition of scripture, that is created using your brain and thoughts. Thus, when it comes to positive thinking and renewing the mind, it becomes vital that we recognize the difference between a negative thought and a protective thought. Failure to do so will keep you spinning your tires, cause you to become more frustrated, all the while keeping you further from your desired results.

It is this voice that I refer to that a person can't speak over. If they try, they will just end up in a conflicting argument within themselves. The voice will tell the person through words, or another avenue, a message that says something conveying they are no good. And the person will respond back by saying, I am a good person, trying to convey that they are good. The voice will come back again in either words, or another avenue, and say the same thing. Then the person will respond back again. What will follow as a result of this is inner turmoil. This inner turmoil is exactly what a lack of peace is. With this lack of peace, it will be impossible to achieve a transformed life.

Pain will always catch up to a person in the future. I remember going through what felt like circles in life. I remember feeling like I made the same mistakes in my life two or three times. I remember finding myself going through similar looking problems that manifested themselves through different circumstances. Different people, different places, different circumstances, but same root problem. Looking back on it, there was a reason for this. I had inner wounds that were bleeding deep within me that I never resolved. As a result, I repeated the same mistakes in certain areas of my life. I always found myself living a life I didn't desire, wishing that I could one day reach my dreams.

EFFECTS OF PAIN

As you can see pain will affect us in a number of ways. I want to discuss in further detail the ways pain can affect us, and what those negative effects mean for our lives. I hope by now you are already seeing the destruction that comes along with unresolved pain. Well actually, I hope that you have already figured out the destruction of unresolved pain, and that your life is going exactly how you want it to go. But if it is not, that's okay, I am glad you are reading this book. I trust that you are going to keep seeing the destruction of pain more and more clearly. I hope by the end of the book you will know exactly what to do to eliminate its sting from your life, so that you can start living the life you have always dreamed of. I believe by the end of the book you will know exactly what to do to transform yourself in getting there. So my hope is that if you do have unresolved painful wounds: you will recognize where they stem from, you will recognize how they have been robbing you in your past and affecting your future, and you will know exactly what to do to break the cycle.

One of the first ways pain affects us can be seen in the way it changes our perception. Pain can affect a person's perception by causing them to see things, people, and situations in a way that they might not actually be. If you are the type of person who always sees the negative in every situation, rather than the opportunity in situations, pain may be the thing that is causing that outlook. Let's take someone who has gone through a painful breakup and has been cheated on. If they don't fully heal from that experience, they will be a little bit fearful of the opposite sex when it comes to viewing them as potential partners. They will most likely hold up a wall, barrier, or guard, which will cause them to look more critically at anyone who reminds them of their past painful experiences.

So in the case of a woman who has been cheated on by a man, the guard she puts up will cause her to view all the men she sees in the future as being in the same category as the man that cheated on her in the past. This new judgment that she believes, now becomes her new viewpoint towards men. Which is the second thing that pain will alter; pain will affect an individual's judgments. Without proper healing from the painful cheating experience, she may never date again. With a level of slight healing from the experience, she may date again, but be too scared to be fully vulnerable with the new man, and may never allow herself to be fully known. She may even choose to date a guy that she knows isn't the best match for her. She will lower her standards and date someone just for the sake of dating. She will pick a guy she likes, but isn't fully into, this way if he ends up cheating on her she can say to herself, I never fully loved him anyways. It's a form of protection for her. She thinks that if she doesn't fully commit again to a man, it will mean that she can't fully experience the pain she has tasted once before, and so desperately wants to avoid feeling again. This is now the third thing that the unresolved pain has affected; the individual's choices. In all these cases, the pain is causing her to fear on some level, which is affecting her future growth in the area of relationships. This principle will apply to any person in any area of their life, and their growth will be limited in whatever area the painful event is causing them to hold back in.

In summary, with an altered perception, a person is going to ultimately make choices that are partly driven and motivated out of fear, rather than out of love and freedom. In the example above, if she chooses to never date again, it's clear to see that a motivation of pain has influenced her future choices. Had she not gone through a relationship where she had been cheated on, she would not be making the choice to never date again. This can easily be seen, as when she chose to date the person who cheated on her in the first place, she was content with her choice to date that person. Had she not been content with that choice at the beginning, she would have made a better choice. The only reason she has changed her mind about her ideas of dating is because of the experience that she went through. So it's plain to see how a painful experience results in an altered perception, thus affecting an individual's choices.

As soon as a person gets cheated on, they will automatically put up a wall, guard, or barrier; that is human nature. If this person doesn't deal with the situation and fully heal from it, they will continually find themselves living with a guard up; that is also human nature. It's impossible to not deal with the painful experience and expect the barrier to come down automatically. It's not just being cheated on that will cause these things to happen. With any sort of pain that a person goes through, the first instinctual thing to happen will be for a wall to go up, no matter what the painful experience may be. Because of this wall we put up, we will be more likely to attract people, or situations, which resemble the individuals, or situations, that hurt us in the first place.

It is like any animal's mating call. Let's take birds for example. Different species of birds have a distinct mating call that can be distinguished between species. When one species of birds sends out their own distinct mating call, they are not going to attract a species that is different from their own. Nor will a bird's mating call bring a different animal altogether. A bird's mating call is not going to attract a deer, and a deer's mating call is not going to attract a bird. Each call is distinct and will bring exactly the right species the call is meant for. Likewise, the same principle applies to us as humans. When we are hurt, victimized, and wounded, our unresolved pain will have a frequency to it that will call and attract us to people, and situations, that are going to repeat that same hurtful cycle. Once we fully heal from our wounds, and our walls come down as a result, we begin to attract people, and situations, that are beneficial for us. In other words, when we put up walls because of pain, we portray a hurt call within us where we attract more pain and hurt; whereas when we are fully healed, we project a love call where we attract love and life. When a person hold up walls, they are actually keeping the pain inside that is trying to escape, as well as keeping out the people who are actually beneficial for them in their life. Being vulnerable is not an easy thing to do. I would even go as far to say that it is impossible to do without fully healing from a hurtful experience. So without the proper healing, a person's experiences will be affected. This is the fourth thing that pain affects; pain affects our life experiences.

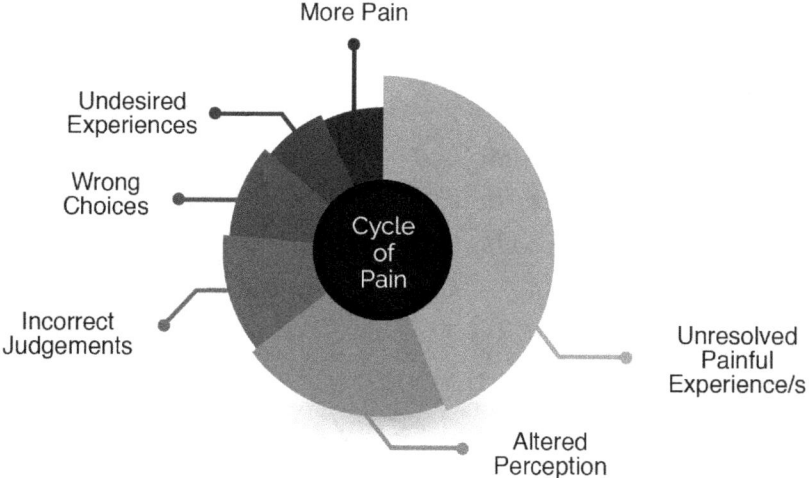

A painful event that is experienced by a person and left unresolved will automatically cause a person to react a certain way. That is, unresolved pain will cause a person to behave in a way that can't be changed without changing the root of the issue. The root of the issue will automatically trigger responses that can't be manipulated, changed, or altered. It's like if I planted an apple tree, I can't alter the tree from growing anything besides apples. All the apples the tree grows will be a byproduct of the apple root. The only thing that I have control over is the root. If I wanted pears to grow instead, I would need to uproot the apple tree, and plant a pear seed. This pear seed will start to form a pear root, which will then ultimately one day produce pear fruit. Likewise, the only way I can change myself from going through the cycle of pain is by making changes to the painful experience that is unresolved in the negative emotional state. If I do not use the right tool to change the nature of the painful experience, I have no choice but to be affected in some way.

The way people treat themselves, and others around them, will automatically change as a result of a painful and traumatic experience that is left unresolved. They may choose to take revenge on either themselves, on other people, or a combination of both. Some people may decide to self sabotage their life. People who choose this option of self sabotage use it as a sort of cop-out. Let's take someone goes through a lot of pain in their childhood. They become so accustomed to believing that life on earth is just a place of pain that they decide to withdraw themselves. Any future situation that has the opportunity for pain to be present, they will try and avoid. Getting a good career, or getting married, may be things that they try and avoid completely. They are scared because these things hold a lot of value and importance to a person's life. In their eyes, going after these sorts of things just presents another avenue where they might end up experiencing more pain. So they may choose to travel, or work jobs without much responsibility, or date people casually. They think to themselves, if I never enter into any serious commitments, then I never have the chance of being let down and hurt. The problem with this is that those things aren't going to bring the desired satisfaction that the person longs for deep inside. It is within pressure type situations where true satisfaction and beauty can be found. If you do a job where you can never make a mistake, or you enter into a casual relationship where breaking up or staying together has no real profound difference, then the chance of greatness, beauty, and love will not exist either.

Diamonds are one of natures most beautiful and precious stones. They are formed under extreme heat and pressure. Before the pressure and heat are applied, all you have is a piece of carbon that isn't that valuable. If a piece of carbon could actually get up and move because it wanted to avoid any pressure and heat, then the beautiful transformation of becoming a diamond would never occur. Diamonds are only created after they experience extreme pressure and heat. The removal of all heat and pressure means a piece of carbon will never experience the glory of becoming a diamond. Likewise, it is the same for people who try and avoid situations in life because they come with too much pressure, or because they come with a chance of being hurt. I'm sorry to be the bearer of bad news, but if you expect to fall into a great career, and/or into a deeply loving marriage/relationship, while at the same time trying to avoid all risks, then you are going to be searching for a fairytale land for a very long time. You will either remain single and jobless, or you will find yourself in relationships and jobs that are not truly fulfilling. This is all because pressure and fulfillment go hand in hand.

This has become very popular among people today, this idea of casual dating. I know of so many people who don't want to enter into a serious relationship. They would rather casually date, or party and sleep around, because they believe it is the best way of protecting themselves from feeling any hurt. But like I said, there is no chance of greatness in these types of relationships, and they will actually end up causing more pain in long run. You can disagree with me if you like, but the more you allow other people to hop into bed with you, and allow others free access to things that are meant to be sacred, the more you will end up feeling less valuable in the end. Its function was to be for one person, to be sacred, and to be shared with someone who understands how precious you are. If you think otherwise, you are free to do so. That is the beauty about beliefs; everyone is entitled to have their own. But if you think you can truly value yourself while also allowing many others to have full access to certain parts of your life, then all the best with that. I hope that makes you happy in the end. I don't believe everyone you meet is going to have your best interests in mind. I believe everyone is valuable, like a precious diamond, and the right person will stick around and wait for you until the time is right. The right person will love you so much and will value you the way you deserve to be valued. But if you don't value yourself in the first place, you can't expect other people to value you either. The way you see yourself is directly linked to the way you treat yourself. People with unresolved pain and hurt will think lowly about themselves. This often results in allowing others to treat you in a way that is less than what you truly deserve.

Another way a person may be influenced by holding onto unresolved pain is through how they decide to treat other people. Some people who get hurt over and over again decide to take revenge on others. When someone gets deeply hurt, they experience a sensation of pain that will obviously make them feel violated and wronged. Since the painful experience that occurred was unjustified, and the person feeling it doesn't feel that a sense of justice was met, they may decide to bring about their own form of justice. This decision to take justice into their own hands is what revenge is. They feel a sense of pain and wrongdoing, and they want to make another person feel the exact same way that they feel. They believe that if they can project and inflict the exact same feelings of pain onto another person, they will then feel better. Needless to say, revenge will never fully satisfy a person's feelings of pain, hurt, and loss. This projection of pain may even drive a person subconsciously, where they find themselves hurting other people without even knowing it. In the next section, I want to share about how I did this exact thing in my relationships, without even being consciously aware of it.

Hurt and pain deep within can manifest itself in a person's life in so many other different ways as well. I just mentioned a few here, but the ways it can take shape in a person's life are endless. I trust you have the ability to look at your own life, to acknowledge, and to be honest with yourself, as to if you have any unresolved pain inside of you; and if so, I trust that you can see how that pain is manifesting itself, and causing you to live your life in a way that you don't actually want for yourself.

At this point, you may be thinking to yourself, I don't want to live a life where I am constantly avoiding the pain that I feel inside. I don't want pain to rule and run my life. I don't want to have my perceptions, judgments, choices, and experiences automatically altered by motivations rooted in pain and hurt. But if I do have any pain within me, what can I practically do to get rid of it? I will cover this in the coming chapters. If you are indeed at that point where you don't want to live your life that way any longer, then you are indeed ready to get rid of it.

PERSONAL EXPERIENCES WITH PAIN

Before I get there, I want to share what I ended up doing in my own life after experiencing a certain painful experience that occurred when I was younger. When I was in my first serious relationship with a girl, I experienced a situation that caused me a great deal of pain. I remember going through it and feeling very hurt by the whole situation. I remember trying to get it out of my mind, trying to let it go, but not being able to successfully do so. I remember what life was like for me after that experience, I felt totally different. I would listen to different genres of music than I was used to, I would drink and party, all trying to get what had happened out of my mind. I eventually started dating again and thought I was over the whole experience.

Fast forward over a decade later in my life. I found myself in a new relationship. Near the end of our relationship, I remember something happening that totally shocked me. I remember the moment very clearly, it felt like I was experiencing déjà vu. During the experience, I remember saying to myself, I feel like this has happened before. I decided to put it in the back of my mind and continued on with life. It wasn't until sometime later that I fully understood what had happened.

What had happened was this. I had experienced a hurtful situation early on in my dating life. I had no idea how to let it go and get over it. I ended up suppressing it as deep as I could within me. I totally thought I was over the whole situation as

I could no longer feel it, and it wasn't something I thought about. Little did I know it still existed deep within my core. Years later I found myself living out what had happened to me, but this time I was the one acting it out. The exact thing that had happened to me years before, I was now living out. I was making another person go through what I had gone through. I call this projected pain. I projected my pain onto another person. I believe that this is one way that pain will cycle around again in a person's life if it is not properly dealt with. When we feel like we have been wronged in the past, we quite often end up wronging someone else in a similar way in the future. That is, we project all the pain and wrongdoing that we feel we don't deserve onto someone else.

I believe that this is one way how pain that is not properly dealt with and healed from can manifest itself again in the future. I discovered that I never fully healed from what had happened because I never properly forgave. As a result, I was never able to fully accept myself and the experience I went through. To be honest, I never actually knew how to properly forgive myself and the experience. Since I never was able to truly forgive myself and the other person involved, I was never able to stop the so called bleeding that kept occurring deep within me. I did a great job of avoiding and numbing that feeling of bleeding for so many years. Looking back on it all, I lived a life of constant avoidance. But it still ended up catching up to me in the end. I couldn't run from it. When I finally wanted to change my life, I realized there was this hurtful voice that played deep within my being. Going to church, reading the Bible, and practicing renewing my mind as I understood it, was not enough to take away this hurtful voice that seemed to play on repeat deep within me. This hurtful voice was affecting the way I lived and the choices I made. It was affecting every area of my life.

When I tell people what I went through, I like to use the analogy of a cassette tape to demonstrate my point. For those of you who are too young to remember what cassette tapes are: they are what people used to play music on before CD's and iPods were invented. At the moment of a hurtful experience, a so called cassette tape is inserted inside of a person. This tape constantly replays over and over again. It can either make a sound that makes you feel down or hurt in your emotions. Or it can play words that we hear in our thoughts that speak negative messages to us. This tape is constantly playing within us. We can try and ignore it by keeping ourselves occupied with something else, but it will remain constantly playing within us.

Usually when a person gets to the point where they want to change their life in a certain area for the better, they will start to hear this tape more clearly. Often times people resort to speaking over top of this tape. This is what most people believe the process of positive thinking or renewing their mind looks like. But no matter how many good things you say about yourself, or how many scriptures you speak over yourself, the tape will keep on playing. Thus, a person will often feel like they are in a constant debate with themselves, and they will find themselves becoming quite exhausted and/or depressed. This is not the correct process for positive thinking or renewing your mind, this is only renewing one's thoughts. True renewing of the mind is taking out the cassette tape that is speaking hurtful and negative things to you, and replacing it with a new tape that speaks positive, uplifting, life giving things to you. Now this is just an analogy, but I really like it because it clearly demonstrates what the problem is, and it clearly demonstrates where we will find our solution. Obviously it is not as easy as opening up your chest, taking out the negative cassette tape, and replacing it with a positive one. If it were that simple, all of us would have already done that by now.

LOOK TO JESUS

So how do we switch this negative tape that plays deep with us? The answer is simple, forgiveness. But what is forgiveness, and how do we practically forgive? This is a little bit more complicated. But in essence, we need to forgive in order to break the cycle of hurt and pain in our lives. Forgiveness is part of what love is. So how do we become more forgiving in our lives? How do we become more loving in our lives?

Jesus. Jesus is our answer. Jesus is our answer for everything. We need to focus on and meditate on Jesus. What most Christians do though is they meditate on Jesus with their thoughts alone. They think of Jesus, they take scriptures and repeat them in their thoughts, and they speak those scriptures out of their mouth. This is a good thing and this should always be done. But it is not the only thing that should be done. We need to meditate on Jesus with our entire mind. That means we need to meditate on Jesus with our emotional state as well. When our emotional state is hurt and negative, that part of us will not be meditating on Jesus. It will be meditating on the hurt and pain. Psalm 1:1-3 talks about the importance of mediating.

Blessed is the one who does not walk in step with the wicked or stand in the way that sinners take or sit in the company of mockers, but whose delight is in the law of the LORD, and who meditates on his law day and night. That person is like a tree planted by streams of water, which yields its fruit in season and whose leaf does not wither—whatever they do prospers.
Psalm 1:1-3

According to these scriptures, the person whose focus is on the Lord day and night will prosper in all they do. Some people interpret this verse to mean they should meditate on God twice a day, once in the morning and once at night. I don't believe this is what this scripture is trying to say. All meditation means is having a constant focus on something. I believe God wants us to have a constant focus on Him all the time. I believe this verse is saying that when we can constantly focus on the Lord all the time, we will prosper in all we do.

You may be thinking to yourself, we all have busy lives, it is impossible to constantly be focusing on God all the time.

But all of us possess a subconscious mind. We can all focus on God in our subconscious mind even while our conscious mind is focused on our other tasks. This is one of the main functions of the subconscious mind. For us, this will be a lot more powerful than trying to make sure our conscious mind is always focused on God. Ultimately we want to have both focused on God as much as we can. This is a great thing to do, and it will benefit us and those around us. But even God knows we have things to do. He knows we have jobs, relationships, and hobbies that are going to require our attention. But even during those times, it is possible for us to have our subconscious mind focused on Him. This is where we are going to experience the most success and power.

The mistake I see most Christians make is they try to compartmentalize their time with God. They go to church Sunday, go back into the real world come Monday, get worn down throughout the week, and need to go back to church the following Sunday to recharge. Others try and spend as much time with God that they can every day. However, when they go to work they have no time to focus on God, so they do what they have to do, then when they have free time again they try to spend as much of it as they can focusing on God. This compartmentalizing of focusing one's attention on God is not what God wants for us. He created us with a subconscious mind for a reason. We all possess a subconscious mind so that we can focus on God 24/7. Focusing on God brings a person peace, joy, and love, as well as many other wonderful things.

God doesn't want us to have to compromise living our lives at the expense of having peace, joy, and love. When we try and meditate on God using only our conscious mind, this is what ends up happening. We inevitably find ourselves having to choose between our time with God and our own life. This is not the proper way of doing things. Our subconscious mind is where we should be meditating on God. When we learn how to meditate on God with our subconscious mind, it becomes possible to focus on God 24/7, and still live our everyday lives. There doesn't need to be a separation. We should still bring our conscious mind back into focus on God as much as we can. In fact, we will want to do this all the more when we truly know how much He loves us. This will be exemplified by going to church, praying, reading the Bible, listening to worship music, or in a number of other ways as well. We shouldn't be doing all of these things to make God love us more, they should be things we love doing because we understand how much God loves us. But I don't want to get to sidetracked here, I just want to illustrate my point that just because you have a task to complete in front of you, it doesn't mean that you need to take your focus off of God.

Let's look at the process of driving a car to further understand this point. Once you learn the basics of driving a car, you don't need to consciously think about using the brake and the gas pedal. You can keep your focus on the road and what needs to be done, while subconsciously using your feet to manipulate the gas pedal, or the brake, to meet the demands of the task at hand. You don't need to tell yourself to push your right foot down harder to speed up, or to apply more pressure with your left foot to slow down. You are subconsciously aware of what your feet need to do. All you need to do is focus on your task and your feet are programmed to assist you along the way. Likewise, we can do the same thing all of the time in regards to focusing, or meditating, on God.

I believe this is one of the main reasons why people don't seem to achieve their desired transformation when it comes to trying to renew their mind. Most people who try and renew their mind only focus on renewing their thoughts, and as a result they are left with a conscious mind focused on God, but a subconscious mind that is not fully focused on God. We need to learn how to focus our emotions and our thoughts on God. Once we are able to successfully do this, our subconscious mind will be able to fully focus on God. And once we are able to do this, our lives will never be the same again.

Take anger for example, if you are focusing on anger in your subconscious mind, no matter how much you focus on happiness in your conscious mind, you will remain angry. Another way to phrase that would be if you are meditating on anger in your emotional state, no matter how much you focus on happiness in your thoughts, you will remain angry. The moment you release the anger from your emotional state, you will be happy. But you don't release anger by manipulating your thoughts. You release anger through certain actions, such as forgiveness. Likewise, we need to release our negative emotional state at that exact same level. We can't keep trying to release it through our thoughts alone and expect to experience a transformation. So now that we all understand what we need to do, and where we need to be making the adjustments, we are ready to learn exactly how to practically release unresolved emotions so that we can successfully transform our emotional state.

FORGIVENESS

CHAPTER 5

Hide your face from my sins and blot out all my iniquity.
Psalm 51:9

So how does a person go about changing their emotional state, that is, how do they renew their negative emotional state in exchange for a positive emotional state? Forgiveness is the answer. Forgiveness is what will bring us out of a life of pain and into a life of love.

When most people think of forgiveness, the first thing they think about is forgiving the people that have wronged them in their past. This is definitely part of forgiveness, and is a step that will always be necessary in order to live freely from the pain others have inflicted in our lives. There is also another major part to forgiveness that I think many people overlook. This part is what I call the justice of forgiveness. I will discuss what I mean by this shortly. But before that, I want to talk about what forgiveness is not.

Forgiveness is not something we our capable of doing in our own strength. We are going to need God's help if we want to forgive others in our life. We are going to need God's love and God's forgiveness for ourselves, before we will be able to give it to other people. Without Jesus' love in our life, I don't believe we will have the motivation to forgive for the right reasons.

I feel like forgiveness is often misunderstood in our society today. I have also bought into the lie of what the world teaches forgiveness is. For some reason, forgiveness gets misinterpreted into meaning forgetting. People think that if they can forget something that has happened, then it must mean that they have forgiven the people involved in the situation or circumstance. This is not true. Forgetting about something is not what forgiving is, forgetting about something is denial. Many people believe if they can just somehow forget about all the memories of the situation, they will be completely free from what happened. So they go about working on themselves, or keeping themselves busy. They keep moving on with life while trying to believe and convince themselves that what happened to them will just go away in the course of time. They believe when it finally goes away, they will have reached the pinnacle of forgiveness. This is not forgiveness, this is what denial is.

Another way to distinguish the difference between forgiveness and forgetting is to judge the underlying motive. A person who is determined to forget a hurtful experience is usually motivated by that exact hurt. Hurt and pain is fueling them instead of love. The reason they are trying to forget about it is because it hurts and it is affecting their future. That is their motivation to try and forget the experience. If the experience didn't cause pain and actually helped their future, then they would not want to forget about that experience. Forgiveness in this case is based out of self-interest, and thus forgiveness turns into this process of trying to forget, which takes away from the true purposes of forgiveness.

Don't get me wrong, with true forgiveness, self-interest is still at play. But freeing and forgiving the perpetrators comes along with your own self-interest. The perpetrators are also important to the individual. In the case of forgetting, the motivation of someone who is trying to forget something, will forgive the perpetrators because it is what they NEED to do in order to achieve their goal of freedom. Whereas in the case of forgiveness, the individual's motivation is based on what they WANT to do; they want the perpetrators to be free to live a better life, where they don't have to keep repeating the same course of action. The individual wants the perpetrators to have the ability to never have to behave the way they did again. They want them to possess the ability to never need to do it again to any other person in the future.

Until we understand God's forgiveness towards ourselves first, we are not going to be able to fully forgive others. *Our ability to love and forgive others in our lives will be based on how much we understand God's love and forgiveness towards ourselves.* The greater we understand God's love towards us, the greater our ability to love ourselves and those around us. Forgiveness is thus a tool, an instrument, something practical that takes us in the direction of love, whereas unforgiveness is a tool and instrument that will take us away from the direction of love. I like to think of it as a vehicle which will take you to one destination or another. Stay in unforgiveness and be taken away from love, be forgiving and enter back into love.

So how do we practically use this tool correctly? Like I mentioned earlier, when most people think about forgiveness, they think about forgiving the people that wronged them in the past. But what does that actually mean? What does forgiving the people who wronged us mean? What it means is you are freeing them from what happened, and you are also freeing yourself from what happened. Since no time machine exists on the earth and we can't travel back in time to change what happened, we are going to need a tool where we can change the course of the past. Forgiveness frees us and the perpetrators from an experience in the past. Becoming free from the hurtful sting of the memories is what forgiveness can do. Forgiveness can't change the fact that it happened, but it can change the feelings and perception associated with the event. I don't believe a person can ever be free from remembering, or being aware of, the events that happened. But I do believe that a person can choose to no longer have it in their focus, and if for some reason it does come back into their focus, the memory doesn't need to be attached to any hurtful, regretful, and shameful emotions. In other words, forgiveness isn't about forgetting what happened, it's about not feeling the sting of what happened any longer.

I understand why so many people end up confusing forgiveness with forgetting/denial, because at first glance they seem very similar. The difference is seen when looked at a little closer. A person who has only forgotten a hurtful experience will feel a change in their emotions as soon as anything related to that experience is remembered. Take for example an ex boyfriend or girlfriend. When you have not fully healed from the relationship, but have just moved on and forgotten about them, then any remembrance of them is going to change how you feel. If you were to be driving in your car and heard a song that was connected to the relationship, then passed the exact make of car that he or she drove, and then passed a restaurant that you went to with them, all of these three experiences would cause a change in your emotions. But a person, who has fully healed and forgiven everything regarding this same relationship, will pass by all of these three things and say something like, that's nice, I hope he/she is doing well. They will not have a change in their emotions because the sting has been fully taken away through the healing they attained through forgiveness.

So now that we know what forgiveness is and what it is not, we are ready to start learning about how to actually practically do it. Like I mentioned before, our answer will be found in looking towards Jesus. So let's start examining Him.

GOD'S FORGIVENESS FIRST

Throughout the Bible Jesus talked about the importance of forgiveness. One of the last things He did before He died was to ask His Father to forgive the people who crucified Him. No matter how much you know about Jesus and who He is, you probably know that His nature and character model forgiveness. Even when the men wanted to stone the lady caught in adultery, Jesus modeled the importance and power of forgiveness.

We learn that under the Old Covenant we are required to forgive first, and then God will forgive us. In the New Covenant, we learn to look to what Jesus did first, and then we draw our strength from Him, and what He did, in order to be able to forgive. Under the Old Covenant it is very difficult, if not impossible, to fully forgive people who have wronged us. Whereas in the New Covenant, we feel so loved and motivated by what Jesus did for us, that forgiveness becomes a natural reflex that we want to do.

Take a look at the difference between these two verses:

For if you forgive other people when they sin against you, your heavenly Father will also forgive you. But if you do not forgive others their sins, your Father will not forgive your sins.
Mathew 6:14-15

Be kind and compassionate to one another, forgiving each other, just as in Christ God forgave you.
Ephesians 4:32

For people who have gone through extremely painful and traumatic experiences, forgiveness isn't the easiest thing to do. To say to them, you better forgive or else God is not going to forgive you, is a very condemning statement. In Mathew 6:14-15, Jesus was teaching the people listening to Him the importance of forgiveness. His motivation was to explain to the people just how important forgiveness is. He wasn't using it as a statement that should be used to condemn people, and pressure them into forgiving against their own free will. His motivation was to bring to light how important forgiveness is for every single human being, so that when they were in a situation of needing to forgive someone, or something, they would look towards Him for strength. He wants us to see that forgiveness is important for our well being and growth as individuals.

We see the verse in Ephesians 4:32 talking about forgiving others as Christ first forgave us. The truth is it is impossible to fully forgive others in our own strength. We need to taste and understand God's forgiveness first, in order to be enabled to then forgive others second. If you try and forgive others first, without understanding God's love and forgiveness towards you beforehand, then you will be left fighting an uphill battle that I don't believe anyone can win. After all, the fact that you are incapable of doing things in your own strength, without God's help, is what being a Christian is founded upon. So forgiveness is also going to go along the lines of that same principle.

If we don't experience God's love and forgiveness first, our desire to want to forgive will not be strong enough. We will be left knowing that we should forgive people, that it is more beneficial to them and to ourselves, but we will find ourselves being unable to act it out. This will actually create even more conflict within us, as we will be aware of what we are supposed to do, but we will not have the capability of living it out.

So if we are going to begin the process of forgiving people in our past, we are going to need to be filled up from God first. Once we know and understand His love and forgiveness towards us, we will then become empowered to forgive others with effortless ease.

FORGIVING OURSELVES VS. FORGIVING OTHERS

So let us begin to look at God's love and forgiveness towards us. When most people think of God's love and forgiveness towards themselves, the first thing that pops into their minds is that He took away the sins of the world. This is indeed true and is a wonderful thing. I am sure you have heard it many times in your life before. When we understand how much we have been forgiven for all the sins that we have committed in the past, it empowers us to want change our lives and live differently in the future. Once you fully understand God's grace and the fact that He no longer holds your sins against you, you are able to experience a sense of love and freedom that is like nothing else found in the world.

If you are reading this book and this is the first time that you have ever heard that Jesus has taken away your sins, I will be very surprised. If it is the first time you have heard this, and you want to understand more about this, there are many great books and sermons on this topic that you can easily find. It would be impossible for me to overstate how amazing and important this truth is about the forgiveness of sins that Jesus attained for us by dying on the cross.

The definitions of sin that I have seen are: an immoral act considered to be a transgression against divine law,[4] the act of violating God's will,[5] and to miss the mark. When people think about sin, they think about themselves and the areas where they do not measure up to what God wants them to do. When a person finally understands where they are falling short, and living in a way that they don't like, they can turn to God and He will forgive them. Technically God has already forgiven them even before they ask for forgiveness, but a person can't receive forgiveness from God when they don't believe they are guilty of anything in the first place. How can someone receive the gift of forgiveness if they believe they are innocent and not in need of forgiveness at all? It wouldn't be possible. So when an individual realizes they are in the wrong, and guilty, that is when they are ready to either look for, or ask for, forgiveness. When they learn that Jesus took away and forgave their sins on the cross, and that He took all of the punishment that deserved to go to them on His own body, they feel loved. That act of Jesus dying for humanity's sins by dying on the cross is an act of love that God was displaying through His Son. When a person understands that, they are then able to forgive themselves for the wrong things they have committed in life.

If you look at the process, God is first demonstrating His love for humanity. Secondly, the minute someone becomes aware of God's love for them, they are empowered to choose to love themselves. In other words, the minute they understand that He forgave them of their sins, is the minute they are empowered to then forgive themselves. It's quite simple and easy to see that God's love and forgiveness comes first, which then empowers the person to be able to love and forgive themselves. Jesus does an action first, dying on the cross, then that action empowers us to take action towards loving ourselves.

But what about forgiving another person? It's great and all to have the ability to forgive yourself for the mistakes you made in life, and the wrongful actions you committed against others, but what about all the wrongful actions that were committed against you? There's no sense in focusing all of your attention on becoming a better person in life, while giving zero focus as to how others are allowed to treat you. I mean, what's the point of growing and expanding yourself, but still allowing others to continue to treat you like garbage. You might as well not even bother growing and expanding if you are going to do that. It would be wiser to digress your growth if you are determined to keep allowing others to treat you like crap, that way at least synchronicity can occur. But as ludicrous as that choice sounds, it seems better than the imbalance many of us settle for. I have no idea why so many of us settle for going to church, spending loads of time working on ourselves, but never spend any time focusing on what is permissible in regards to how others may treat us. To me this seems like a very unhealthy balance. I'm not sure exactly where it stems from, but I feel many people have a misunderstanding of what true humility actually is. Many people have this misconceived notion that the more you let other people walk all over you, the more humble it means you are. Reciprocally, the more you take care of yourself and don't settle for certain things, the more arrogant it means you are. This is completely backwards. When a person is walking in true humility, there will be a sense of confidence in the individual that others may mistakenly perceive as arrogance.

Before I get too far off track, let me get back to the question we were asking before. How do we practically forgive other people, especially people that have hurt us in the past? Well depending on how you look at it, you can't. It is impossible to forgive someone else. Before I scare all of you, what I mean by this is that you can't forgive anyone else on your own. You need Jesus' love and forgiveness first, then you will have the ability to forgive others. Just like you needed Jesus' love and forgiveness before you were capable of forgiving yourself, you are going to need Jesus' love and forgiveness before you can be enabled to forgive other people. So how do we understand and receive Jesus' love and forgiveness? Just like in our solution before, we need to look to what He did on the cross. He took away our sins on the cross, so our answer to being able to forgive other people will also be found by looking at what Jesus did on the cross.

This is the part that many people seem to either forget, or be unaware of; the part about what Jesus accomplished on the cross that is going to empower us to forgive other people. Not only will this part empower us to forgive other people, it will empower us to forgive ourselves at a deeper level, which enables us to be able to love ourselves on an even deeper level. For some reason Christians have the tendency of only focusing on the fact that Jesus took away our sins. This is only part of what Jesus accomplished by dying on the cross, all be it a really amazing part. I can see why so many Christians focus on this part, as it is so mind blowing and amazing. But since He paid for so much more on the cross, wouldn't it be silly to not focus on the other things as well.

I could write an entire book about all of the other things that Jesus purchased for us on the cross, all of the other things that he died to give us, in addition to the forgiveness of sins.

I could have done that, but I already see plenty of books like that in the book store already; books which are wonderfully written and have a lot of great information for the reader to take in. But for those people that know me, I'm sure "unique" would be an adjective they would use to describe me. So I wouldn't have been passionate enough to write a book about something that I have seen someone else write on before.

The reason I wanted to write this book was to share with other people what I learned about, in regards to something Jesus died for, that I feel barely gets talked about and mentioned. I feel this part is vital in understanding and focusing on, as it is the part that helped me transform my own life. Even more than that, it took me from a negative emotional state, to a positive emotional state, in the snap of a finger. The part I am referring to is iniquity. Once I got a revelation of what iniquity meant, it transformed my entire life. I went from being depressed and unable to forgive people in my past, to being able to forgive them completely. I also was able to love and accept myself in a way that I had never been able to do in all my years of living. As soon as I got a revelation of what iniquity was, what it meant to me, and how it related to Jesus, my life was instantly transformed.

What I discovered and learned about iniquity motivated me to write this book. If you are like I was, you probably have no idea what the word iniquity even means. However, I believe it is something Christians need to understand, if they want to experience transformation in every area of their life. Who doesn't want to have the ability to transform their entire life? Who doesn't want the ability to fully be able to forgive themselves and others! I believe once a person fully understands what iniquity is, and how it relates to Jesus and the Bible, they will possess all the practical things that they need to know in order to transform every part of their life. I trust the next chapter will be a blessing to you, and to everyone connected to you in your life. I look forward to hearing about all the testimonies of your transformed lives.

OUR ABILITY TO **LOVE AND FORGIVE** OTHERS IN OUR LIVES WILL BE BASED ON **HOW MUCH WE** UNDERSTAND **GOD'S LOVE** AND FORGIVENESS TOWARDS OURSELVES.

INIQUITY

CHAPTER 6

The meaning of iniquity is a gross injustice or wickedness. It can also mean a violation of right. In Latin the word is inīquitās, and it means unevenness or unfairness.[6] The point I was working towards last chapter in regards to sin is that most people's few first thoughts when they think about sin is related to the sins they have committed in their own life, either towards themselves, against God, or against other people. For some reason the sins other people have committed against us get pushed to the back burner.

When it comes to iniquities, I feel we do the exact same thing. We think of the injustices we have committed towards other people in our past. We think of all the uneven and unfair ways that we ourselves have treated other people in the past. I don't think this is a bad thing to feel remorseful about. I think it would be quite unhealthy if we had the ability to misuse and abuse people, and actually feel good about it. But my point is that we shouldn't solely think of what we have done wrong to others. We need to be aware and acknowledge the times in our lives where we were wronged. I am sure everyone can think of a situation where they were treated unjustly and unfairly. Maybe you have been cheated on in a relationship, maybe you have been sexually abused, maybe you were abandoned as a child, or maybe your parents went through a divorce, any one of these things happening to you is grossly unfair. They are injustices. There are so many more experiences that someone could have gone through that I could list, besides these four examples I wrote down. There are so many examples of situations that can cause a person to experience injustice. If there was an experience that occurred in your life that deeply hurt you, and deeply wounded you, then it is an injustice. It is what the Bible refers to as an iniquity.

For some reason, Christians don't seem to focus on this side of the coin. We think about all the injustice we have done. But when it comes to the injustices that have happened to us, we seem to not focus on them, or even talk about them. Let's take the example of sexual abuse. Obviously for people that have been sexually abused, it is not something they are going to want to focus on all the time. It's not something a person wants to keep reminding themselves of. However, at the same time, it is not something that you want to completely ignore either. As we saw in the last chapter, ignorance, or denial, isn't what true forgiveness is. Having a healthy balance is extremely important. If a person who has been sexually abused is on either side of the extreme, it is going to be hurtful and harmful for them. If they think and focus on the event that happened all of the time, it is going to hurt deeply, and it will prevent the individual from ever healing from what happened. But if they go to the other extreme, and never think about what happened, then that is going to be extremely unhealthy as well. They will end up living a life of denial and never receive the healing they deserve to get, since they need to acknowledge the wound first, before they can even begin to receive the necessary healing. Everyone deserves to be healed, to feel complete, and to feel like they are worthy. Jesus died for all of humanity, and there isn't one single person who is too unworthy of His unconditional love.

Remember the story of the person with the bullet wound I talked about before. They want to have a healthy balance in regards to their solution. If they get shot and constantly look at the fact that they have been shot, they are going to go crazy with fear and anxiety. If you have ever needed to go to emergency for a serious wound, you will probably remember that either the ambulance driver, the doctor, or the person helping you get there, will try and calm you down by taking your attention off of the injury. They will try and get your focus off of the wound, so you will not go into extreme shock, or get too overwhelmed.

However, imagine you finally get in to see the doctors and they tell you, "It's all good. Everything will be okay. What I want you to do is not focus on the wound, and if you can do that long enough, it is going to heal itself. If you find yourself thinking about it, right away make yourself stop. If you can successfully do this, then the wound will be healed." This extreme is obviously not going to heal the wound. It's easy to see the fact that proper healing will not occur in this example. The same exact principle remains true when it comes to our past hurts and so called bruises. Thinking about them all the time is not healthy, but neither is ignoring them and not thinking about them ever. Outer wounds will never properly heal with these extreme solutions I just mentioned. Likewise, inner wounds will never fully heal unless we have a properly balanced and precise approach. Precision and balance is the key. We don't want to be using an imbalanced solution that actually makes the problem worse in the end.

CAN BAD THINGS HAPPEN TO GOOD PEOPLE

Before we can even see what our precise solution is, we must settle something else for good. If this is not fully settled in our minds, we are not going to be able to experience the required healing. We must break this lie from the enemy. I myself used to be guilty of believing this exact lie. I don't know where this lie gets its origin from, but I can clearly remember when I actually believed it to be true. What I am talking about is this idea of bad things happen to bad people and good things happen to good people. This is such a destructive lie that comes from the pits of hell. When people believe this statement to be true, then every hurtful experience they face in life, or that they went though in their past, they will believe that they must of somehow been responsible for it.

You see this when people talk about karma. They are unhappy with an experience and you will hear them say things like, "I need to behave differently in the future so that it doesn't happen to me again." What is at the core belief system of a person who says this is a statement that says, good things happen to good people and bad things happen to bad people. This is an absolute lie. It can be planted inside of a person's mind and become a belief, and they will never be able to escape its destruction if they don't change their mind and put in a truthful statement.

How can it be true that someone who was sexually abused when they were a small child be at fault? How can children be at fault when their parents decide to get a divorce? How can a baby who gets abandoned be at fault? They can't be! They couldn't have behaved better, or performed better, in order to change the fact that the injustice occurred. For some reason people have a hard time believing this. I remember I used to have an extremely difficult time getting rid of this lie. Every time I went through something traumatic in my life, part of me felt responsible, like somehow something had to have been partly my fault. I am here to tell you that is an absolute lie. Bad things can happen to good people. However, good people don't need to let the bad events affect them; they have the ability to forgive.

This is a much more healthy statement to hold than believing that bad things can only happen to bad people. Because if you believe a statement like this, then every time you remember something that occurred that was hurtful to you, you will think that it must have been your fault somewhere. You will think that the injustice that you experienced must have been partly your fault. If you believe this, then you will be more focused on trying to make sure you are better in the future so that something like that will never happen to you again. Whereas when you realize the experience was an injustice, you will begin looking for the necessary steps regarding healing. Like I mentioned earlier, once you experience the proper healing, it will free you up to live a life of contentment, full of freedom and wholeness. This will cause you to attract more healthy people in your future, and push hurtful, unhealthy people away.

Until a person is able to change their thinking and replace this lie with the truth, it will be impossible to find the proper healing, since the solution for healing requires a person to admit they were fully wronged. In other words, a person will not be able to receive God's healing from something traumatic if they believe they are partly responsible, because as we will soon see, God's solution for healing can't be seen unless a person admits to the fact that they were fully wronged. So if a person can't see God's solution for healing, how do they expect to receive healing? That would be like trying to receive forgiveness of sins from Jesus without ever recognizing and admitting that Jesus existed. You can't believe that Jesus took away your sins while also believing that Jesus is made up, and is not real. That is impossible. Another way to phrase that would be: it is impossible to receive forgiveness of sins from Jesus without knowing Jesus. Likewise, it will be impossible to receive forgiveness and healing from the iniquities committed against you, if you don't believe they were iniquities.

This principle is just common sense. It may be a little confusing, so let me tell a story to drive home the point. If you have a cut on your leg, but you're unaware that it is there, and I come to you and offer you a Band-Aid, you will reject receiving it from me because you don't realize you need it. Once you see that you are cut, you will believe that you are cut, and if I come to you and offer you a Band-Aid, you will receive it from me because you realize you need it. This is what I mean when I say *it is impossible to receive something while also believing something doesn't exist*. That is exactly why I stated that it is impossible to receive healing from the iniquities committed against you if you don't believe they were indeed iniquities.

Let us remember what iniquity is. It is a gross injustice, something that was unfair and uneven. If you feel that you were responsible for something that happened to you, that there must have been something that you did that caused you to deserve a hurtful event, then you can't at the same time fully believe it was an injustice. Either the hurtful event was warranted in coming into your life because of something you did, or the event wasn't warranted, it happened to you for no reason. It was fully wrong, therefore it was an injustice. It's impossible to have both statements remain true. That is exactly why I said before that until we change our thinking and believe that hurtful things can happen to good people, without a justifiable reason, we won't be able to receive the full healing God wants to desperately give us.

If you still are not convinced that bad things can happen to good people and without a justifiable reason, let's look towards a place where we can find the truth. Let's look toward the Bible. What does the Bible say about this topic? Who do we look at for our answers for what is true? Jesus. A quick look at Jesus' life and we will see the truth right away. Jesus was a perfect man, without sin. In other words, He never did anything wrong. Bad things happened to Jesus. He died on the cross, He was spit on, and He was insulted; I could go on and on. We can't say these things happened to Jesus because He did something wrong. That would be untrue. But these things still happened to Him. Bad things happened to Him and He was a good person, in fact, He was a perfect person. Jesus couldn't say to Himself, if I would have done things better, then maybe those bad things wouldn't have happened to me. The reason He wouldn't say that is because that entire statement isn't from Him. It comes from the enemy.

The truth that He showed was that bad things do indeed happen to good people. But just because they occur, it doesn't mean they have to defeat the person. There is a way to be undefeatable no matter what hurtful stuff can come your way. He is that way. What He represents is that way. He never got defeated on the cross, He rose back to life. He was resurrected. He forgave every single person that was responsible for putting Him up on that cross. That forgiveness was part of the love that He represents, and that forgiveness was part of the reason He was resurrected. Forgiveness holds the power to never let anything defeat us. Unforgiveness is a poison that will only hurt the people who drink it. It doesn't actually destroy the people who hurt you in the first place.

A PLACE OF EXCHANGE

There was a reason Jesus died on the cross. There was a reason He took on all this hurt on His body. That reason is so that we will have a place where we can also put our hurts. Jesus dying on the cross acts as a place of exchange. Like I mentioned earlier, the exchange that many Christians seem to focus on the most is the exchange of sins. The things we have done wrong in our lives. The things we have done to hurt ourselves and others. Every human being has the choice to give Jesus their sins, and in exchange He will give them life, love, forgiveness, and freedom. That alone is quite a glorious thing. I can see why so many Christians focus on that. When a person does that, and experiences the love of God and the freedom that comes with it, it is enough to keep them feeling so thankful for the rest of their lives. But like I also said earlier, that is not the only thing Jesus died and paid for, so that we as human beings can exchange things we don't want, for things we do want. God is a great God, and He is so generous. He could have stopped at just that gift -- the forgiveness of sins -- and we would have been so thankful, but since He is so generous, He wanted to give us so much more.

We see in the scriptures some of the other things He gave people when He walked the earth. He gave sick people health.

There are so many scriptures telling us about the healings that He performed. There are stories of the material blessings that He performed. Like Peter finding money in the mouth of a fish in the book of Mathew. Peter needed money to pay the temple tax, and Jesus gave it to him.[7] Jesus also gave so much more than just healing and material goods. Like I said, I could write an entire book about all that He provided. He loved humanity so deeply, and so desired to be able to provide a way for all of humanity to be able to receive from Him, that He sacrificed Himself on the cross so that we can always go to Him. For the people in the 21rst century, He wasn't planning to still be walking around the earth for that long, so He died on the cross, so we would still have a place to go to if we wanted to receive things from Him. It's such good news, and that is exactly why it is called the gospel.

So we see that Jesus, and His death on the cross, is a place of exchange. It's a place where we can go to give Him things we don't want anymore, and receive things that we do want. Isn't that what we are trying to do with the past hurts that have been committed against us? If your parents got divorced, if you had been abused as a child, if you had ever been abandoned, are you not trying to get rid of the pain and hurt that was afflicted upon you? Of course you are. No right-minded person loves going through those experiences. Even people who believe they are responsible for the hurtful experience coming on them are trying to change their behavior in the future, for the sole purpose of hoping that their improved behavior will prevent painful experiences from ever happening again. It doesn't take a rocket scientist to know that people don't like pain and hurt, and that when someone experiences situations that cause those feelings, they will try all the solutions they know of to try and get rid of those feelings. I have good news; you can give them to Jesus. For some reason, we as Christians have forgotten the fact that we can give the hurts caused to us to Jesus. We seem to only ever focus on giving Jesus the hurts and wrongs we have caused other people. That's only half the equation. There is a whole other side of the coin that has somehow been forgotten, where we can do the exact same thing with the pain, hurt, and wrongs done to us. How do we do this? What are the practical steps we need to take in order to give this to Jesus? Our answer is, iniquity, and how iniquity relates to Jesus.

INIQUITY EXCHANGE

Like I said, people seem to always quote a scripture that mentions how Jesus took away the sins of the world, how Jesus took them on His body, and how His blood has paid for them once and for all. There are many scriptures that you can find that talk about this that you can look up. A few of them are found in Romans 6:23, 1 John 1:7, and Romans 5:8. This is a glorious truth and should never cease to be something people worship God for. But it would be even greater if we could combine our worship over the forgiveness of sins, with all the other glorious parts about Jesus.

The one part in particular that I feel Jesus doesn't get glorified enough for, is the iniquity that he bore on his body. I'm not sure people even fully understand what it means for us, that Jesus bore our iniquities. In Isaiah 53:5 we read:

But he was wounded for our transgressions, he was bruised for our iniquities: the chastisement of our peace was upon him; and with his stripes we are healed.
Isaiah 53:5 (KJV)

We can see that Jesus was bruised for our iniquities. Jesus was bruised for any gross injustice, any unevenness, and any unfairness. This does not only include the acts that you have committed against other people. It also means that Jesus was bruised for all the unjust, uneven, and unfair acts committed against you, inflicted by other human beings. As Jesus died on the cross, He experienced bruising on His body from all the physical blows that He took. These blows obviously caused His body to bleed, and it is with this blood that we have the access to receive His healing. The Bible mentions this in 1 Peter 2:24.

"He himself bore our sins" in his body on the cross, so that we might die to sins and live for righteousness; "by his wounds you have been healed."
1 Peter 2:24

And we see in Galatians 3:13:

Christ redeemed us from the curse of the law by becoming a curse for us, for it is written: "Cursed is everyone who is hung on a pole."
Galatians 3:13

Jesus redeemed us from all the curses that are mentioned in the Bible, by becoming a curse for us. In Deuteronomy chapter 28, you can find the blessings and curses that a person can receive. Under the Old Covenant a person needed to behave perfectly in order to receive the blessings from God. If they did anything wrong and sinned, then they would experience the curses that are listed in that chapter. One of these curses is sickness. A person who wasn't fully obedient in their behavior towards God could experience any number of these curses, including sickness.

Thank goodness that is the Old Covenant God had with man. Under the New Covenant, all a person needs to do is believe that Jesus took on all the curses on His own body, and redeemed us from the curse of the law. By the wounds Jesus took on His body over two thousand years ago, we have been healed. Notice the tense of the words, we have been healed. We're not trying to get healed, we already have been healed. All that is required now is for us to believe it, and to manifest it in our lives. If we have cancer, we believe that Jesus took up cancer on His own body, and therefore it would be double jeopardy for us to experience cancer also, since He already paid the price for cancer. If we believe that He has already paid the price for it, then we can give our cancer over to His body, and receive from Him healing. We can exchange the cancer we are experiencing by giving it over to Him, and in exchange we can receive our health. Just like sin can be exchanged for forgiveness, so can our sickness be exchanged for health. We just need to believe what the Bible says. You may be asking yourself, how then do we practically believe? That is a great question! I will cover this question in the next chapter.

Jesus' body was wounded for our healing according to 1 Peter 2:24. In the same way that Jesus was wounded for our physical healing, he was also bruised inside His body for our emotional healing. Isaiah 53:5 captures this truth by telling us that Jesus' body was bruised for our iniquities. So not only was Jesus' body wounded, and the blood that flowed afterwards became our solution to healing our bodies, but his body was also bruised, and the blood that flowed inside of His body became our solution to healing our inner wounds.

The difference between a wound and a bruise is seen in where the problem is occurring. A bruise is where the injury occurs inside of the body, where the skin is not penetrated, whereas a wound starts on the outside of the body and penetrates the skin. Basically, wounds form on the outside of the body, whereas bruises form on the inside of the body.

Jesus' body was indeed bruised for our iniquities according to Isaiah 53:5. That means Jesus was bruised on the inside, and He shed blood on the inside of His body. Now this same blood will be what heals us from the inner wounds that we carry inside of our bodies. These bruises we carry are the wounds of our heart; they are the pains we carry inside of our negative emotional state. They are the wounds that I refer to as bleeding deep within us. These are the wounds that cause us pain, grief, and shame. They end up controlling our life. That is why they need to be healed from. They need to be set free. If not, they will drive us and control our life.

How we go about healing these inner wounds will look similar to the way we heal our outer wounds. We will look to Jesus, and look to His blood that has already been shed over two thousand years ago. Pontius Pilot ordered Jesus to be whipped and flogged by Roman soldiers. You can read about this in John 19:1, or Mathew 27:26. I am sure you are familiar with plays or movies that portray Jesus' back being repetitively whipped while He was tied to a whipping post. The Bible says that with all the wounds that Jesus bore on His body, the blood that shed out of them became our healing. Anyone therefore who believes this, has the right to receive healing in their life from sickness and disease. Throughout the process of Jesus dying on the cross -- that is, from Jesus being in the Garden of Gethsemane up until He was resurrected -- He experienced several other blows to His body, including wearing the crown of thorns, and receiving several blows to the head, just to mention a few. You can read about these two things in Mathew 27:29-30. Like I said before, I am no doctor, but I do know that being forcefully struck on the head with an object is going to cause some bruising inside. It's obvious that Jesus' body was bruised in the process of going to the cross, and the Bible makes sure to make it clear to us in Isaiah 53:5, telling us that His body was indeed bruised. So just like the blood Jesus shed through the wounds He received from all of the lashes He took heals our diseases, so will the blood Jesus shed from the bruises He experienced while dying on the cross heal our emotional pains. In other words, the blood that Jesus shed inside of Himself will become the healing for all of our emotional pains, wounds, and hurts.

When we are bleeding in our insides, it means that we are bruised somewhere deep within us. We have wounds on our hearts, which affect our emotions. These wounds also cause pain and hurt to our mind and soul. When someone goes through a traumatic experience, they are going to have wounds that form within their mind and their soul. These wounds are going to need a release, or they will prevent a person from flourishing and blossoming into the life that they desire.

So how does a person get rid of inner pains and inner hurts? The same way they get healing for their diseases. They look towards Jesus. I mentioned earlier that when someone goes through a painful experience, a new voice will start to come alive inside of them. It will remind them of a hurtful experience. It will make the individual feel like they are not valuable because of the fact they had that experience happen to them. The voice will always try to haunt the individual by bringing their focus back to that event. What people often tend to do in this situation is bottle up this feeling and this voice inside of themselves. They try to ignore and suppress it as deep as they can until they don't feel it any longer. This is a very serious mistake, as it will either explode in the future, or it will cause the individual's life to follow along that same path, where they will end up repeating a similar cycle in the future. There must be a healthy release of this voice, the pain, and the hurt, or it will be detrimental to the individual trying to manage it.

In order to understand how to practically release all this pain, we need to do a few things first, or we won't be able to actually see the proper solution and know how to carry it out. First, we must recognize that there is a wound inside of us in the first place. If we don't acknowledge and recognize the wound, but instead try and ignore it, we won't move towards finding a solution. Next, we must understand that the wound within us is something that is detrimental to our success. We must understand that a wound left untreated, will lead us in a direction that will be unbeneficial to our overall health and success. After we realize there is a problem, and we make up our mind that we want it fixed, we will be ready to see the solution, and be able to live it out.

If you haven't caught the drift yet after reading through the first 5 chapters, our solution will not be solely positive thinking/renewing our thoughts alone. That is going to have no effect on changing the wounds that bleed deep within. We need to renew the wound that bleeds deep within. So how do we actually practically do this? We need to look at what the scripture actually means that states Jesus was bruised for our iniquities.

We read earlier in Isaiah 53:5 that Jesus was bruised for our iniquities and the chastisement of our peace was upon Him. These two things are going to be major keys. Later in Romans 4:7 we read *blessed are they whose iniquities are forgiven, and whose sins are covered.* (KJV) The Bible mentions that a person who has their iniquities forgiven is blessed. I don't need to comment on the fact that we all desire to be blessed. So how does one get from carrying iniquities in their life, to having them forgiven, thus being blessed? The simple answer is we need to give them to Jesus. But those are just words. How do we actually give them to Jesus? I am going to explain how we can give them to Him next.

I find statements like that limiting. Like how I said, you need to give them to Jesus. Saying the statement does not actually do anything for another person. In doesn't help them become enabled to successfully do it. It's like when you tell people the phrase, Jesus loves you and He forgave you of your sins. They look at you like you are crazy. It doesn't change the fact that Jesus loves them, and that He did indeed take away their sins, but the phrase has no meaning to the person hearing it. If they one day in the future realize that Jesus does indeed love them, and they realize that He has taken away their sins, then that phrase will have meaning to that individual. But if the phrase has no meaning to someone, it is not going to do them any good hearing it. They need to feel that Jesus loves them, rather than just hearing a statement that says Jesus loves them. So if you make someone feel loved by showing them love, and at the same time tell them, "Jesus loves you, and He forgave you of your sins," then that statement is going to have meaning to the person hearing it.

Likewise, there is no use in me telling you to give your iniquities to Jesus if I don't show you how to actually do it. It's one thing to know what to do; it's another thing to actually be able to do it. So to understand practically how to give your iniquities to Jesus, you are going to need to know what iniquities are, how they relate to Jesus, and how you can practically exchange and get rid of them. I've already covered what they are earlier and I began to explain how they relate to Jesus. Let's continue looking at how they apply to Jesus, and let's continue working towards understanding how we can practically get rid of them. Because as we can clearly see, the Bible mentions that those who have their iniquities forgiven, and their sins covered, are blessed.

FULLY GOD, FULLY MAN

We know that Jesus was fully God and fully man. The Bible tells us this is true in Hebrews 2:14-17. This is extremely important in working towards seeing our solution.

Since the children have flesh and blood, he too shared in their humanity so that by his death he might break the power of him who holds the power of death—that is, the devil—and free those who all their lives were held in slavery by their fear of death. For surely it is not angels he helps, but Abraham's descendants. For

this reason he had to be made like them, fully human in every way, in order that he might become a merciful and faithful high priest in service to God, and that he might make atonement for the sins of the people.
Hebrews 2:14-17

We see two important things here. First, we see that Jesus was fully man and fully God at the same time. The second thing we see is that by Jesus' death, death gets defeated. Since Jesus came and died, death no longer has power over any of His children. I am sure you have heard in church, or somewhere else, that if you believe in Jesus, you attain eternal life. Part of the meaning of eternal life is the fact that death can no longer occur again. Hence, it has been defeated. We see that there is power in Jesus' death. The same thing goes for any fear and emotional pain. Through Jesus' death on the cross, they also get defeated. For some reason we as Christians always focus on the fact that Jesus died and we now have eternal life, but we never give any focus towards the fact that fear and emotional pain was also defeated through His death. If you ask me, I think we should be focusing on the whole package. It would be silly to be blessed with three children, but only focus on one of them. So likewise, if Jesus died for more than one thing, it would be silly to pick just one of them to focus on, while ignoring the rest. So how did Jesus' death actually take away our emotional pain? Let's begin to examine that.

Since Jesus was fully God and fully man, He possessed all the qualities and abilities God possesses, and He possessed all the abilities and qualities that human beings possess. God is omniscient, meaning that He can be in two places at once. It also means that He has the ability to be aware of everything. Human beings possess the ability to feel pain, to feel emotions, and to have thoughts. So since Jesus was fully man, He was able to feel the emotion of anger, or experience the feeling of shame. In fact, He was able to experience all feelings and emotions.

There is a reason the Bible states that Jesus was bruised for our iniquities. There is an important revelation related to this fact that God wants us to see. God is trying to demonstrate and reveal just how deep His love for us truly is. He can't just say that He loves us deeply without any actions backing up that statement, because as the Bible shows throughout history, His children always questioned and doubted the validity of that statement. The kind of deep unconditional love that God has for us is so revolutionary and mind blowing that it can't solely be expressed through words. The limitations of words and language can never capture and grasp the infinite love that God has for humanity. It's impossible to do.

That would be like me coming to you and asking you what your best friend was like. You could take me for coffee for an entire year and describe to me all the ins and outs of your best friend. After a year I would obviously know a little bit about them. If we continued meeting for another entire year, I would continue to learn a little more about them. But if I decided to scrap the coffee meetings and actually spend one day hanging out with your best friend, and I got to know them, that one day of experiencing their presence face to face would tell me a lot more about who they are, than I could ever learn about who they are through you telling me. My point is that your best friend is indescribable through words alone. Words and language have limitations. The point of words and language is to try and describe an experience. *The experience of something will always be greater than someone's description of that same experience.* Experiences speak louder than words.

Maybe you are familiar with an experience in life where you felt like you were at a loss for words. Or maybe you have seen other people say a phrase like, "I can't express what I am feeling right now in words." This often happens after a sports team wins a championship and they are asked to describe how they feel. It can also be seen in a romantic relationship where one person can't quite find the proper words to describe to their partner how they feel, and portray to them just how much they love them. The reason is because your experience of the emotion that you are feeling is indescribable.

I would not say God does not have the capability to create the words to tell us just how deeply He loves us. But I would say that we are limited by our humanness to be able to understand such glorious and infinite love. Therefore, if we are going to be able to understand the love God has for us, we are going to need to experience it. Just hearing words, without having an experience behind it, will profit us little. That is why God decided to send His Son Jesus, so that we could have access to experience His love.

So back to where I was when I said there is a reason why Jesus was bruised for our iniquities. Jesus wants us to know just how deep His love for us is. So He decided to come and die for our sins, as well as all the hurtful things we may experience in this life from others, all to demonstrate His love for us. He didn't want to just come to earth and tell people that, He wanted to take action to prove that also. And this is exactly what He did by going to the cross. This is the part that I feel so many people in the church today are unaware of. It has so much power, and it can set people free from so many things, but we are not aware of it. Since we are unaware of it, we never begin the process of focusing on it. Because we never focus on it, we never begin to ponder it. Because we never ponder it, we never begin to meditate on it. Finally, because we never meditate on it, we never see the fruit of it in our lives. This is an extremely powerful thing we can focus on as Christians. For most of us when we worship, we focus on the fact that Jesus died for our sins. This is a great thing and it brings glory to God, all the while uplifting us. But when we start worshiping God for this part about iniquities also, it will help us see God's love for us in a whole new way. When we finally start doing this, we will experience God's love at a much deeper level.

Again, on the cross Jesus took on all injustice, unevenness, and unfairness inside of His body. In His mind, and in His soul, He experienced all the injustices ever committed against human beings. It is mind blowing to me the fact that God Himself cared about me so much, and loved me so much, that He decided to feel everything I have ever felt in my lifetime on His own body. How glorious! How marvelous! Our God decided to use His omniscient power -- His ability to see everything from the beginning of time until the end of time -- to know every painful event that His creation may experience in their lifetime, and then chose to experience those exact hurts in His own body, mind, and soul. He loves us so much that He decided to come and experience all hurt on His body, so that He would be able to relate to us.

Not only did Jesus feel every painful human emotion, He insisted on doing so. We see this fact by looking at the significance of the wine mixed with gall, which was offered to Jesus on the cross. This account is captured for us in both Mathew 27:34 and Mark 15:23.

There they offered Jesus wine to drink, mixed with gall; but after tasting it, he refused to drink it.
Matthew 27:34

Then they offered him wine mixed with myrrh, but he did not take it.
Mark 15:23

Many historians tell us that this drink was used in Biblical times for the purpose of sedation.[8] That is just a fancy way of saying it was used as a painkiller. This was the morphine of the day. From the verses above, we see that as soon as Jesus became aware that what they were offering Him was a painkiller, He immediately spit it out. One of the reasons

Jesus refused to take a pain-killing substance was because He wanted to make sure He felt all of humanities painful experiences. He wanted to feel, and fully experience, every single individual's painful experiences. He didn't want a watered-down experience of the pain we feel. He wanted to feel it identically to the way we feel it. Hence, this is why He spit out the painkiller, as taking it would have alleviated some of the pain. He wanted to experience our exact pain. He wanted to experience our exact iniquities. That is, He wanted to experience the full measure of all the unjust, all the unfair, and all the uneven acts that are committed against you and me. He wanted to demonstrate just how far He would go to know us that intimately. How amazing is this fact, God Himself wanted to know us and accept us so much, that He sent His son Jesus to die for not just our sins, but also for all the wrongful injustices done to us in this life.

Not only did He do all of this so He can relate with me, but He did all of this so that if pain ever happened to me in my life, I would have a person I can unload all the damaging emotions on. That means, if I was ever in a relationship and a girl cheated on me, Jesus Christ knows exactly what it is like to be me, and to be cheated on. He loved me so much that He decided to come and experience that hurt on His body, so that He would be able to relate to me, and so that I would have a way to deal with it. Rather than needing to hold onto all the scars my entire life, I would have a way to be able to give Him all the hurt and pain, if I chose to do so. He loved me so much, that He didn't even force me to give Him my pain and emotional hurt. If I wanted to keep the scars and wounds formed inside of my mind and soul from being cheated on, I could choose to do so. But if I didn't want to hold onto them any longer, I could give them to Jesus, and release them from my life. The exact moment in time I no longer want to carry them, is the exact moment He will gladly receive them. Not only is this for the painful experience of being cheated on, but for any hurtful injustice.

If I have been raped, if I have been abused, if I have been abandoned, if I have experienced a divorce, whatever the injustice may be, I could release them by letting Jesus take what He has already paid for. That just absolutely blows my mind! Jesus loves me that much that He would do all of that for me. The same goes for every single human being.

If any of you have ever been raped, if any of you have ever been abused, if any of you have ever been abandoned, if any of you have ever been divorced, if any of you have ever experienced your parents go through a divorce, Jesus Christ decided to come die on the cross and feel all of those experiences inside of Himself at every level. Any wrong doing that can happen to a person in their life, Jesus said, I am going to come and take that all on. I am going to experience all those circumstances in my body. It will be as if it were happening to Me. What love! If a person ever wants to let go of the sting and hurt of any painful memory, they can give it to Me. He knew that people wouldn't be able to give their painful experience to Him, if He Himself never experienced them. They would be stuck having to deal with it on their own. They would be stuck having to carry that burden, that shame, that pain, and that wound inside of them for their entire life. So He decided, I am not going to have that. I am not going to leave people having no way of getting rid of their hurtful experiences. What I am going to do is come and die on the cross, and experience the fullness of their painful experiences. So if they ever want to get rid of the pain, they can stop carrying it by giving it to Me. In exchange for their gift of shame, hurt, or any burden they will ever have, I will give them love, acceptance, value, wholeness, contentment, and belonging. Jesus thought, I will give them my love, my life, and my wholeness, if they want to give Me their burdens. I love them way too much to not provide a way for them to exchange such things. So I will be the way. And any person who chooses to can come to Me, and they can freely receive from Me.

Are you serious! Jesus loves us that much! When I learned this, it absolutely blew my mind. It was so blown that all of the pain and hurt I had ever experienced my entire life was completely gone. It died with Jesus on the cross. I was left feeling whole, complete, valued, and accepted. All my emotional baggage and scarring was gone. I no longer felt that so called inner bleeding. It was as if it never happened. It obviously still happened, the pains in my life still occurred, but it was as if they were no longer part of who I am. I had completely forgiven myself, and the people that hurt me. I had completely let them go. Looking back on it, I can see that this is what forgiveness is. This is what forgiveness was all along. I spent so many years in addiction, using other people, trying to numb and avoid that emptiness I felt inside.

I convinced myself that if I can just forget about that feeling, that emptiness, it would mean that I had finally reached the pinnacle of forgiving. I learned that this was completely backwards.

JUSTICE

In order for a person to fully forgive somebody, justice needs to be part of the process. In the Bible, our sins and wrongdoing needed justice. God will always be a just God, it would be unloving if He wasn't. There is a penalty and punishment that needs to be paid for sin. In the Old Covenant a person's behavior had to be perfect, the minute their behavior was not perfect, they were guilty of breaking laws. Since laws were broken, punishment needed to occur. That is why much of the Old Covenant covers things that God's people could do to make atonement for their misbehavior. It wasn't until Jesus came that God provided a way for the punishment to be transferred from you to Him. Jesus became punished and judged for everything we deserve to be punished for. That is why He is referred to as a Savior. And this is why the Bible mentions He is the One that atones for our sins. If you go to some churches, they force fear down your throat and tell you that you will go to hell if you do something wrong. If you asked most people on the street, this is the stereotype about Christianity. Indeed sin is not something that you want in your life, as it has many consequences. But as for punishment, God took out all the punishment of humanities sins on the body of Jesus Christ. If God didn't punish Jesus, and just forgot about our sins, then that would be a very unjust and unloving thing for Him to do. So Jesus paid the punishment that we deserved so that we would not have to pay it. This way justice is served for all the wrongdoing.

In order for a person to experience restoration in their life, justice needs to occur beforehand. Before a Christian is able to experience the forgiveness of sins, they need to acknowledge that Jesus took away their sins. Without that acknowledgement, they will feel personally responsible for all the judgment and penalties of sin. They will be left feeling they are the ones that need to pay the price. In the Old Testament, through the story of Noah, we see this example of justice being met before restoration occurs. The flood had to come first, as a form of justice, before God could bring the earth into a state of restoration. We can see many other examples of this principle throughout the scriptures. Justice will always need to occur first, before a form of restoration can occur second.

When it comes to our painful emotional wounds, the same principle applies. We are going to need justice before we can be restored back to our lives, back to the way they were created to be lived. When someone is wronged and unjustly hurt, the natural response will be a longing and hunger for justice to be served. This isn't hard to see, all one needs to do is look at our judicial system. Its whole function is to provide justice when wrongs have occurred, and the system does the best it can at creating punishments that line up with the wrongful act committed. I'm no expert lawyer, but I do know that stealing a chocolate bar might get you a fine, and most likely not a night in jail. But if you steal from a bank, or if you steal a car, then the punishment is going to increase since the act is deemed more severe. The principle of justice coming first, in order for the victim to feel restored, is one of the main functions of why courts exist. Justice is vital and essential. Without it, restoration becomes impossible.

In the same way, justice needs to be part of what was done wrong to each of us. If painful and hurtful things happened to us and there was no form of justice, then that would be very unloving of God. God also knew this, and this is exactly why Jesus took on His own body all the pain and hurt that we can experience in our lives. Jesus needed to be punished for all the injustice that has happened to you. If not, we would try and get justice back by ourselves, by either hurting ourselves, or hurting others. He knew we would either try to project our pain onto other people, or try to numb and avoid the pain by suppressing it. This is what people turn to doing with their pain and hurt when they don't give it to Jesus. Without Jesus, if an individual goes through a painful or traumatic experience, they will be left trying to forgive and move on from it on their own. I myself did this for many years, with absolutely no success. I bottled up my pain deeper and deeper until I became depressed. As a result, I became scared to let anyone get to know me. I became someone I was not proud of. I became ashamed of myself and who I believed I was. As a result, I treated everyone in my life in a way that they did not deserve. This all stemmed from who I believed I was, and how I treated myself.

If a person has no way to release the hurt, pain, and scars which occurred in their life, they will be prevented from living life to the fullest. That is why I believe it is so important that we start focusing on this part regarding what Jesus died for us to have. If you go to any church, you will hear about the fact that Jesus took on your sins, or that Jesus forgave you of your sins. But when is the last time you were in a church where they told you that Jesus accepted you even with all the wrong and hurtful things that have happened to you? That Jesus accepted you so much, despite whatever wrongfully happened to you in the past. That He wanted you to know that He loves and accepts you so deeply, that He even experienced whatever painful situations you went through. He didn't want you to feel alone. He didn't want you to have no way of releasing hurts. So He took it upon Himself to go and die on the cross and experience all the injustices you have tasted in life. So that when you no longer wanted to carry the hurtful baggage, you could exchange it with Jesus for love and acceptance. It is time that we as a body of Christ start focusing on the entirety of what Jesus paid for by dying on the cross. It's time we start praising Jesus for the fact that He was bruised for our iniquities and that He died for our sins. If we continue to only praise Jesus for the fact that He died for our sins, we will be left loving Him for only one of His amazing attributes. We will never become more intimate with Him if we only understand and focus on part of who He is. We want to move towards understanding who He fully is.

As we saw earlier in the book, lack of fullness is a dangerous thing. Our lack of fullness, in regards to our understanding of who Jesus fully is, has held back the body of Christ. In the next chapter, I will discuss how this has held us back from fully trusting in God, and how this lack of trust has affected our lives.

BELIEVING

CHAPTER 7

When I go to any church, I always see so many people wanting to receive things from God. There are a lot of blessings that God promises His children in the Bible. In fact, every time I go to church I see people wanting to receive something from God. Who in their right mind wouldn't want to receive something wonderful from God, it's a no-brainer. If you are sick and slowly dying from a deadly disease, who wouldn't want to receive a healing touch from God. If you are struggling in your finances, who wouldn't want to experience the abundant life that God promises. If you don't have peace in your life and inside of your body, who wouldn't want to receive the peace that surpasses all understanding that God promises. I have never met a person who doesn't want to receive something great from God; that usually isn't the issue. But what I do see are people who do not understand exactly how to practically receive things from God. Many of God's promises hinge on the fact that we need to believe them. So how do we practically believe God? What do we need to do to believe? I want to look at this idea of believing God and examine what it actually means. After all, if receiving things from God requires us believing, we should know exactly what to do in order to be able to believe.

What most people end up trying to do is muster up enough belief in God in order to be able to receive something from Him. They know that all the promises in the Bible hinge on the fact that belief is necessary for them to receive them, so they try to create as much trust and belief that they possibly can. They think that trust is something they are solely responsible for. They think that once they have built up enough trust, belief, or faith, they will be finally ready to receive the promises they know God has stated. This is totally backwards. Trust and belief is not something a person can manufacture, nor is it something they are solely responsible to manufacture on their own.

The problem with this idea about trust and belief is that it puts you at the center of fueling and creating it. Most people will read the Bible as much as they can, they will go to church as much as they can, and they will pray as many times as they can, all hoping that these actions will increase their level of belief. They think that if they are able to do this enough times, then finally they will be ready to receive from God the promises that they desire. I often hear people say things like, "I need to read my Bible more," or, "I need to go to church more often." I always think to myself, no, you need to fall in love with Jesus more, then you will want to read your Bible more, and you will want to go to church more.

For some reason people have this idea about faith, belief, and trust being a one way street. It is true that we are responsible for believing God, believing His word, and believing His promises. But it is not true that we are solely responsible for creating all this on our own. God has a part to play in this process as well.

I always like to think of the things of God in terms of how I see and picture a relationship. In any relationship, you aren't required to fully believe and trust your partner at the beginning. You want to have a good healthy balance in your trust levels. You don't want to give your date zero trust, and have your guard up completely, that will not be helpful in deepening the relationship, nor will it allow you two to get to know each other better. On the other hand, you don't want to ignorantly give your complete trust to a person who you hardly know. That could become problematic as well, as there are certain things you wouldn't want to experience with that person until you knew them better. So it's best to trust them accordingly. Then as the relationship matures, more trust will be earned as they prove how much they love you. It's not up to you to solely manufacture all of the trust. *Both parties have a role to play in building and growing the trust.*

Likewise, it is the same with God. First, you begin a relationship with Him. Next, over the course of the relationship you learn to understand Him more, you learn more about who He is, and what He has done for you. Then finally, when you realize how great He is and what He has done for you, your trust and belief will have grown automatically. In your relationship with God, trust and belief are not solely your responsibility. It's not up to one side to provide all of the trust and belief to help facilitate love to grow. Both you and God have a role to play. The mistake I see most people making is misunderstanding the balance in this relationship. It's time we learn to do the things God wants us to do, and leave the things that God is supposed to do, up to Him.

So what are the parts that we are responsible for in this relationship, and what are the parts that God is responsible for? That is a great question! Let's start to unpack all the goodies in that question and begin to grow our understanding. After all, we should know exactly what we have to practically do in order to execute our faith properly.

This reminds me of something I learned from the years of being a tennis instructor. For those of you who don't know tennis, the point of the game is to hit the ball over the net and into the court on the other side. It was my job to make people who came to me better at being able to do that. Now if one of my students was constantly hitting the ball into the net, there is no use in me going up to them and telling them to hit the ball over the net. They are aware of the fact that the ball needs to go over the net. What they are not yet aware of is all of the techniques that they can use to effectively get the ball over the net. Therefore, it's pointless for me to repetitively tell them to hit the ball over the net. There is no power behind that statement. But if I teach them the techniques needed to successfully hit the ball over the net, then when they subconsciously tell themselves to get the ball over the net, they can then turn on the necessary mechanisms needed to achieve that goal. Like I stated earlier, it's one thing to know what to do; it's another thing to actually be able to do it.

This brings me to the problem I see so often in our churches today, that problem being people being taught what they should do, but never learning how to actually do it. It's one thing to say in church you should forgive your spouse when they get mad at you, but it's a whole other thing actually being able to do it. We spend so much time in church learning about what to do, but we don't spend much time learning how to do it. In my eyes, the practicality of the 'how too's' are more important than knowing what to do. Back to my tennis example, I know what I need to do to beat Roger Federer in a tennis match, but I don't possess the skills to actually be able to do it. I know that if I hit shots in the corners, never make any mistakes, and run down every shot that he hits to me, I will beat him in a match of tennis. But to actually be able to do all of those things is a different story. If I was actually in the heat of the moment, that is, in an actual tennis match against him, I would not be able to execute all of those things that I know I need to do to beat him. It's obvious to see that execution is harder than just simply knowing what to do. Likewise, knowing that we need to have faith in God is one thing; actually being able to execute the proper skills necessary to activate faith is a whole other thing. Like I just stated, this is the problem I see with our churches today. Most people going to church know that they should not get angry with their spouse when they do something that hurts their feelings. But actually being in the heat of the moment when they hurt you, disappoint you, and make you angry, is a whole other ball game. Actually being able to forgive them and show them love back, instead of hurt, is a skill that can't be taught through head knowledge.

There is a difference between knowing something and being able to execute something. I have been building up to this point throughout the entire book. Being something is different than saying something, or knowing something. I have used the example of anger through this book. When you are angry with someone there is only one way to turn that anger into something else. It is impossible to constantly repeat positive phrases that work towards trying to convince yourself that you are happy, only becoming happy will work in your efforts to become happy. The same thing goes for showing your spouse forgiveness. You can't expect to only have head knowledge about forgiveness and execute the required techniques of forgiveness when the situation calls for it. The more important thing that underlines all of this is being forgiveness; in other words, having a forgiving nature. The role of a church is to teach people to become forgiving and loving natured. It is not to solely teach them what they should do to act forgiving and loving. These things are good to learn, but they pale in comparison with knowing how to possess that kind of nature.

Before I get too far off track, let me tie this all together. The question we were asking before was how do we practically believe? How do we practically have faith? This is one of the hardest questions to answer. People for centuries have been trying to answer and understand this question. I don't actually think this question has an answer that can be described in words. We have been conditioned to think of faith in terms of trying to grasp it and understand it. I believe this is exactly why we have yet been able to define it. Belief and faith will automatically flow out of a person when they meet the proper requirements.

That brings me to the first point about faith. There is a proper balance to faith that needs to be understood. This balance often throws people off because it is something that is counter intuitive to what is considered the norm. Our relationship with God, and the promises of God, all come in the form of a gift. This is why I feel so many people get thrown for a loop. The only way you can become disqualified from receiving a gift is by trying to do something to get it. The minute you try and do something to earn a gift is the exact minute you disqualify yourself from receiving a gift. A gift can only be a gift when there is no action taken on the other side. There are two parties at play in the exchanging of a gift. There is a giver, and there is a receiver. The giver can only give a gift when the receiving party decides to receive. The receiver can only receive when they trust the giver. This wanting to receive, and trusting the giver, is what we are responsible for when it comes to our role in faith. Wanting to receive is a free will choice that can only be decided on by the receiver, they hold the final say. However trusting the receiver is a two way street. Both the receiver and giver have a part to play in this process.

When it comes to receiving, we are responsible for getting ourselves out of the way. This is where most people struggle the most. Most people have a very hard time accepting a gift that has no strings attached to it. Most people feel this urge to have to do something in order to deserve a gift. As soon as they feel this way and decide to take a step of action, they become ineligible to receive. You see, the only requirement in receiving a gift is maintaining zero qualifications. As soon as you qualify to receive a gift, you become ineligible to receive it. This is because your actions of qualification have turned the gift into something that is now owed. That after all is the definition of a gift: something that is given for no reason whatsoever, besides the fact that the giver wanted to express love. I feel we as a society have forgotten the true essence of what receiving a gift means. It's time we remember how to receive again.

Since receiving things from God come in the form of gifts, it is essential that we learn how to receive. Like I said, there are many blessings and promises in God's word. When we are in the way, it automatically disqualifies us from being able to receive them. One of the main things that hinder us in this process of receiving is our unresolved pain and hurt. The reason for this is because our past hurts that go unresolved start to create doubt within us. This doubt will then counteract our ability to successfully believe, which will directly impact our ability to receive.

DECREASING DOUBT

Doubt is the only thing that will directly affect one's ability to be able to believe. Most of us don't have an issue with our believing; most of us have an issue with unbelief. Jesus knew the power that doubt had when it came to the arena of faith. He knew that doubt was the only force that could slow down the supernatural workings of the Kingdom of God. We see this principle modeled to us in the book of Mark through the story of Jesus raising Jairus' daughter from the dead.

While Jesus was still speaking, some people came from the house of Jairus, the synagogue leader. "Your daughter is dead," they said. "Why bother the teacher anymore?"

Overhearing what they said, Jesus told him, "Don't be afraid; just believe."

He did not let anyone follow him except Peter, James and John the brother of James. When they came to the home of the synagogue leader, Jesus saw a commotion, with people crying and wailing loudly. He went in and said to them, "Why all this commotion and wailing? The child is not dead but asleep." But they laughed at him.

After he put them all out, he took the child's father and mother and the disciples who were with him, and went in where the child was. He

took her by the hand and said to her, "Talitha koum!" (which means "Little girl, I say to you, get up!"). Immediately the girl stood up and began to walk around (she was twelve years old). At this they were completely astonished.
Mark 5:35-42

We see people coming to Jairus and telling him, it's too late now, your daughter is dead. But Jesus responds back by saying, "Don't be afraid; just believe." Jesus knows that being afraid represents doubt, and it will counteract belief. Later we see Jesus entering Jairus' daughter's room. But before He performed the miracle of raising her from the dead, we see that He put all the doubters out of the room. Only the child's parents, and the disciples that were with Jesus, remained in the room. After doing all of this, He proceeds to raise her from the dead. We see the principle I am talking about here of doubt being a power that will hinder the miraculous. Jesus knew full well that doubt will short-circuit belief. This is exactly why He put the people crying and wailing out of the room. So when it comes to transformation in our own lives, we are going to have to believe God, which means, we are going to have to get rid of any doubt that we have in our life. I explained earlier in the book that it is impossible to believe and not believe at the same time. I can't think I am a loving, amazing, and wonderful person, while at the same time also believing I am a no good, terrible, and disgraceful person. It's like that analogy I used to describe keys fitting inside of a door lock. I can't fit two keys into a lock at the same time. Only one key will fit in at a time. If I have one key inserted in the lock, I am going to need to take it out before I can insert the other key. The same thing goes with our beliefs, I can't successfully hold onto two opposing beliefs at the same time, it is impossible to do.

Likewise, when we hold onto unresolved hurt and pain, it's impossible to hold onto healing and joy. Unresolved hurt and pain will make us feel ashamed and worthless, where as resolved pain will make us feel loved and accepted. It's impossible to hold onto both of those things at the same time in a certain area. Most of us have unresolved pain and hurt residing in our minds. This causes major problems to our overall health and well being. This problem in the area of our minds needs to be released and healed from if we desire to experience emotions of love and acceptance. It's quite obvious what most people want and desire. Most people don't desire to feel hurt and broken, that usually isn't the issue. The problem is that they don't know how to transform those feelings into the feelings that they do desire. So they end up using all the techniques they know about to try and get the job done. However, I believe there is only one way to fix such a problem. That is, you need to give them to Jesus so He can gift you back love. But like I said earlier, these are just words. Actually being able to practically exchange your pain with Jesus, and use the proper and precise techniques, is a whole different story.

What most people have learned, and are still often taught to do, is to try and renew their mind. This is the correct way of dealing with the problem. However, most people's understanding of what renewing their mind looks like is incorrect. Most people have learned this misconception about the principle of you have what you say. It is indeed true that you attract what you say, but there is more to it than just this. The way most people view this principle is incomplete. The truth is that you will have what you say provided that you believe what you say. For some reason many people forget this extra little bit. But it is this extra little bit about also believing what you say, that makes all the difference in the world.

This applies directly to a person's unresolved inner wounds that they carry inside of their negative emotional state. Another way to say their negative emotional state would be: their mind, their heart, their soul, or their subconscious. For the sake of understanding, I am going to refer to one's subconscious mind to clarify what I mean. Many people have unresolved pain that exists deep within their subconscious mind. They can sense that it is there, and they sometimes become courageous enough to try and do something about it. The process and tool that people often turn to is increasing their positivity. People think that this will automatically increase their faith. They start trying to muster up as much faith that they possibly can to try and change what is going on inside of their subconscious mind. What they do is they fill their conscious mind with as much faith and belief that they possibly can, hoping that the increase will be able to override what is going on at the subconscious level. However this won't work, and it causes quite the problem.

What ends up happening is they believe in their conscious mind, but they doubt in their subconscious mind. They trust God in their conscious mind, but they don't trust God in their subconscious mind. This ends up causing an internal conflict. This internal conflict is what the Bible refers to in James as double-mindedness.

But when you ask, you must believe and not doubt, because the one who doubts is like a wave of the sea, blown and tossed by the wind. That person should not expect to receive anything from the Lord. Such a person is double-minded and unstable in all they do. **James 1:6-8**

James tells us that a double-minded person can't receive anything from God. Notice what he refers to as being double-minded: a person who believes God, while at the same time, part of them doubts what they believe. This is what I mean when I refer to a person trying to believe God in their conscious mind, but they have their subconscious mind working against them by producing doubt. The double-minded person reflects doubt and we just learned earlier that doubt is the one thing that will cancel out belief. So we know that we want to avoid being double-minded at all costs, unless of course you aren't interested in receiving God's wonderful promises.

The internal argument that a person inevitably ends up in through double-mindedness, will rob them of their peace.

The reason this argument occurs is because in their conscious mind they believe that God loves them, and that He wants to give them the promises they have been believing for, but in their subconscious mind they perceive God as someone who can't be trusted. It's human nature for your subconscious mind to go into defense mode after a painful experience. The only way to get out of this, and stop this inner conflict, is to reveal to your subconscious mind that God does indeed love you, and that the perception of God being someone who can't be trusted, is not true.

Why does the subconscious mind tell a story of God not loving the individual? The reason for this is because this is where all of a person's hurt and pain is stored. When someone goes through a traumatic experience, all the memories, emotions, and feelings will be stored in one's subconscious mind. This is where the root of the problem will be found. So unless they experience God's love for them at this exact level, no amount of hearing about His love, or repeating scriptures that tell them about His love towards them, will do them any good. It is only the experience of God's love that will heal the wound that a person holds in their heart, mind, soul, and subconscious.

Any painful and traumatic experience that a person goes through will cause them to ask themselves something along the lines of, "Why did God let this happen to me? If God was really in charge, I would have never experienced this." These are questions of doubt, not trust. I am sure you can hear the doubt built into the question as you read it. Being able to answer this question in one's subconscious mind will be the only way an individual can release painful wounds. If we do not find an answer to this question, it will automatically cause us to hold onto doubt at the subconscious level. So we need to experience God's love, and understand the justice in the wrongful acts committed against us, before we can forgive and truly heal. Furthermore, we need to be able to truly heal before we will be able to receive anything from God.

Think about it; remember I said the only stipulation required for receiving something from God is belief. Belief is going to require trust. You are not going to trust God if you think He is the One that is responsible for you going through a traumatic experience. Many people think to themselves, "If God was in charge, then that means the horrific act actually occurred, and God did nothing to stop it." They think that God has done nothing to protect them from experiencing that act, and that He has done nothing to bring justice to that act. This is not true. This is why we need to understand the part about Jesus dying for our iniquities.

ACCEPTANCE

I don't know why we only focus on the fact that Jesus died for the sins we have committed against others. We need to understand that Jesus also died for the iniquities committed against us as well. If we are not aware of this, we will have no way of feeling justified for a painful event that has occurred against us in our life. If we never feel justified from a painful experience, we will never be able to forgive the people that committed it against us. More importantly, we will never be able to forgive ourselves. If we can't forgive ourselves, we will never be able to accept ourselves. We will always feel deep down that we are damaged goods. We will feel dirty, shameful, disgraceful, and unworthy.

One of the deepest human longings is to feel accepted, to feel like you belong. We can never successfully get rid of this longing; it is part of our makeup and DNA. When we get scarred from a painful experience, this longing does not go away. The reason many people turn to revenge is because in their eyes it satisfies that longing of belonging. If someone gets abused and they don't forgive and heal from it properly, they will want to project that pain onto someone else. This projecting of their pain will make them feel justified in the fact that now someone else knows what it is like to feel like them. It's human nature to be known, understood, and accepted. Jesus knew that if He never took on people's unjust and painful experiences, then it would mean that they would have no place where they could exchange it in a healthy way. That is why he chose to feel all the exact pain that humanity could experience on Himself. He did this so that they could give their pain to Him, and in exchange He could give them love, joy, value, and acceptance. Like I mentioned earlier, He even refused taking the painkiller, of the wine mixed with gull, which was offered to Him. He made up His mind that He was going to take the punishment set before Him, and experience all the torture of all of humanities painful experiences.

For some reason Christians only seem to focus on the fact of what they did wrong to other people, but there are two sides to the coin. We need to glorify God for all that He paid for on the cross, and this includes the iniquities that were committed against us. We need to understand that whatever the unjust, unfair, and uneven acts that were committed against us, those same exact acts were also committed against Jesus Christ on the cross. Once we become aware of this truth it enables us to accomplish many wonderful things.

First of all, it allows us to fully experience God's love for us. When you understand that He loves you that much, and you exchange your baggage with Him, in exchange for love and newness, it frees you to live the life that you have always desired to live. The acceptance and value that one feels after understanding just how much Jesus cares for them, frees them from all the fear and worry that has held them back in the past. God's acceptance is something we all long for, and only Jesus can fill that longing.

The next benefit that comes, through exchanging our hurt and pain for Jesus' love, is the ability to get rid of the voice that people try to silence through positive thinking, and their idea of renewing one's mind, but are never able to successfully do so. In the next section, I want to go into further detail about this inner voice.

CHASTISEMENT

When someone goes through a painful and traumatic experience a voice will come to life deep within that individual. The voice asks the question, "If god truly loved you and valued you, why then did you go through that painful experience." Many people do not have an answer to respond back to this voice deep inside their subconscious mind. So since they don't have an answer, they try and silence it by speaking over top of it with as much effort that they can in their conscious mind. This is not the correct process to renewing one's mind. The correct process involves renewing the emotions and feelings inside of one's heart as well as renewing the thoughts in the brain. Most people miss this step and only focus on renewing their thoughts alone. However both of these areas need to be renewed and work together. It's like rowing a boat, if you only use one oar, and only row on one side, you will just keep spinning in circles.

I mentioned earlier in the book an analogy of a cassette tape playing deep within a person's negative emotional state. What I was trying to describe was a voice playing deep within one's heart, mind, soul, and subconscious. If you have a cassette tape speaking negative words that is inserted inside of you, it is foolish to try and speak over that cassette tape with positive words that contradict what the tape is saying. The cassette tape won't stop playing negative messages just because you say positive messages. It is much wiser to eject the cassette tape and insert a new tape that speaks life giving messages. That way when you hear the tape play, the words you hear will uplift you, and you can come into agreement with what is being said. That is what true positive thinking and renewing the mind is. It's about replacing the negative tape with a positive one. It's not about manufacturing as many positive messages that you can to say over yourself in your conscious mind, while a negative tape plays deep within you in your subconscious mind. Let's bring our awareness back to the verse in Isaiah 53:5.

But he was wounded for our transgressions, he was bruised for our iniquities: the chastisement of our peace was upon him; and with his stripes we are healed.
Isaiah 53:5 (KJV)

The word chastisement means to rebuke, or criticize severely.[9] This is the voice that I am referring to that comes to life when a person goes through a painful and traumatic experience. It is impossible to get rid of this tape, this pain, this wound, and this chastising voice, by speaking over top of it. Only healing from the pain will suffice. If we could just open up our bodies, hit the eject button to the tape, insert a new tape, and then go on our way, our problem could be easily solved. But it doesn't work that way. The only way to get rid of this so called tape, and receive a new one, is by exchanging it with Jesus. The only way we can exchange it with Jesus is to understand that He took on our painful unjust experiences, including the chastising voice that comes along with it. On the cross Jesus was tortured and was being tormented by all the painful and traumatic experiences that you and I will ever go through.

This is how we then eject the negative tape that plays inside of us. We eject it, and allow Jesus to take it for good. This is done by acknowledging that He did this for us and that this scripture is indeed true. As soon as you come to this step of admittance, He offers you a new life giving tape that speaks words of love to you. He won't force this tape on you, nor will He take the opportunity away from you to receive it. No one is disqualified in this matter, regardless of who you are, what you have done, or what you have gone through. But until one realizes that they need this tape, and that they want it, nothing can be done. Remember the story about the Band-Aid, it's just like that. If you are cut, but don't realize you are cut, you will not receive a Band-Aid from me if I come to you and offer you one. It's not that I don't want to give you a Band-Aid, and it's not that I don't care about you healing your cut, it's that you can't receive a Band-Aid from me if you don't realize you are cut, and/or if you don't want one.

When we go through a painful experience we are going to hear a voice that chastises us and tries to say to us, "If god truly loved you and valued you, why then did you go through that painful experience." We need to be able to answer this question. The truth is that God loved you so much that He wasn't actually the One responsible for the hurtful event happening to you in the first place. The voice might phrase the question like, "If God truly loved you, then where was He when you went through that painful experience." We also need to be able to answer this question also. The truth is that God loved you so much, that He was on the cross experiencing the exact same painful and traumatic event that you went through. No matter the painful experience, Jesus knows exactly what it is like to feel that same pain.

When you go through a painful breakup, you can't just go to the doctor and ask them to give you a new heart that isn't broken. A breakup is not a reflection of a physical problem with your heart. The doctor sending you into surgery and performing a heart transplant will not fix your problem of a broken heart, even if the new heart that gets donated comes from someone that never experienced a breakup in their life. A broken heart caused from a painful breakup is a spiritual and emotional problem. Therefore, the solution has to come in that area also. Jesus Christ is a healer of spiritual and emotional problems.

Like I mentioned throughout this book, He acts as a sort of exchange. Most people are familiar with the exchange of sins that can be given to Him in return for eternal life. But that is not all Jesus Christ offers people. He also is the One who we can exchange our brokenness with. So if we do have a broken heart from a breakup, we can exchange that broken heart with Him in return for a new healed heart. This new heart we receive in return will not forget about the event of the break up completely, but it will take away the sting of all the painful and hurtful emotions.

This is why the Bible tells us that *he was bruised for our iniquities and the chastisement of our peace was upon him.* (KJV) Jesus didn't take on our iniquities and the chastisement of our peace for no reason. He knew that He had to take on our painful experiences, and the voices that criticize us afterwards. If He did not, then we would have no way of moving on from them and letting them go. So this is why He decided to experience all the negative voices that you and I may hear after a hurtful experience. He became cursed with all the damaging emotions, so that we would not have to experience them, if we decided we didn't want to.

We wouldn't be able to exchange our pain and hurt with Jesus if He never died and paid for them. Like I stated earlier, trusting in God is something that needs to be felt and experienced, it can't be manufactured. It's impossible to feel and experience full trust in God when painful events remain unresolved deep inside of a person. Those hurtful events do not speak life, nor do they grow a person's trust. We need to give the pain to Jesus and let it die on His body, that way it will no longer have any authority and power to exist in our life. In other words, all of the sting from the pain and hurt we have experienced in life, needs to get transferred onto Jesus' body as He died on the cross. When we do this, it will be put to death through His death, and thus it will have no ability to live in our bodies, in our souls, and in our subconscious minds any longer.

You may be thinking to yourself, this seems too farfetched. I can't just transfer things from my life onto Jesus' life, and cross through the barrier of time. But isn't this exactly the same thing we as Christians do with our sins. Don't we transfer our sins onto His body, even though He died for them over two thousand years ago! That's the foundation of what being a Christian is based on. So if you don't believe that is possible, then I don't know how you could call yourself a Christian in the first place. But if you do believe that is possible, then it isn't much harder to believe what I am saying. If you believe your sins can be transferred from your life onto Jesus, the same amount of belief and effort is required to believe you can transfer your iniquities onto Him as well. So I trust that you have the ability to do it, and to free yourself from whatever traumatic experiences you have gone through. I trust you can transform your life, and start manifesting the life you always longed for, dreamed of, and deserve to be living.

FOCUS

What has your focus been on? I know what it is like to live a life where everything you dream of always seems so far away. I spent every single year of my life in this state, except for this last year. Deep within me I was focused on pain and hurt. I thought that was just the way life was supposed to be. I became so accustomed to letting people down in my life, and being let down by the ones closest to me. I found myself living in a way where I was always wishing I was somewhere else. No matter what I did for work, it was never fulfilling enough. I would constantly dream of living a different life. It always seemed so far away, always just out of my reach. I pushed the people I dated away, because deep down I was too scared to let myself be fully known. I could go on and on about all the things I was unhappy with and depressed about. I would always ask people this one question, what is the one thing that is worse than death? I knew the answer. I lived the answer! Living, but never truly being alive; living just to exist.

When you live life, and the idea and thought of death seems better than your current state of existence, it is a sad thing. Life is meant to be enjoyed and lived to the fullest. We all deserve such a beautiful life. When we carry deep, painful, and hurtful wounds that remain unresolved, it becomes impossible to be truly vulnerable, to take risks, and to live life to the fullest. We need these painful wounds recognized, acknowledged, dealt with, and transformed, through true forgiveness. We need to give them to Jesus. We need to exchange them for His attributes, so we can live vulnerable, free, and without constant fear. Then we will be able to transform our lives into the life we long for and dream about.

This experiencing Jesus' love for us in the area of our painful experiences can't be created in any other way. This love He gives us from this process is what fuels a person's transformation. There is no other avenue that successful transformation can properly occur through. Often times I see people who try and create this sense of love for themselves. They try and convince their conscious mind that God indeed loves them. They tell themselves over and over again, I trust God, and God loves me. I trust God, and God loves me. I trust God, and God loves me. They may even start to quote scriptures over and over again to themselves, trying to reach a satisfactory level of convincing themselves to believe God. Can you now see the problem that might arise here? Trust is not something that can be manufactured, it needs to be something that is felt and experienced. It is not true that you are solely responsible for growing all your faith, and trust, in your relationship with God.

People get so caught up trying to believe God that they make it much more complicated than it needs to be. Most people's solution to creating more belief is trying to mentally assent themselves into it. Most people who are familiar with positive thinking and renewing their mind are used to the process of constant repetition. They are taught that if they keep repeating something, usually a phrase, for long enough, then what they have been saying will eventually come true. But this is not the correct way to increase one's belief levels. This process actually causes a person to unknowingly enter into a state of denial. One cannot change the emotion of anger with the constant phrase of, "I am happy." One needs to feel they are happy to actually be happy. I think this stereotype comes to people from what Jesus said in the book of Mark.

Truly I tell you, if anyone says to this mountain, 'Go, throw yourself into the sea,' and does not doubt in their heart but believes that what they say will happen, it will be done for them. **Mark 11:23**

This verse says if you say something and not doubt it, but believe it, then you will have what you say. It does not solely say you will have what you say. It mentions there are a few other factors at play, doubt and belief to be specific. For some reason many people believe they can manipulate themselves into believing what they are saying to be true, and that if they repeat what they say long enough, it will eliminate all their doubt. This is not true, and like I just mentioned, it will bring a person into a state of denial. There needs to be a connection to what you say in your words with what you feel in your heart. If you feel one way in your heart, the only way to change that would be to change the emotions of your heart. After you successfully do this, the words you were saying before to try and convince yourself of something will actually bubble out from within you. Changing your subconscious mind's thoughts, feelings, frequencies, and vibrations, is what true positive thinking is.

If you got in a fight with your spouse and you became angry, it would be silly to walk away and spend a full week meditating and telling yourself, "I am happy." A week later in time you will still be angry! But if at any moment in time during that week you come to your senses and decide to go to your spouse to resolve the issue, as soon as the issue is worked out through understanding, or forgiveness, you will instantly feel happy. As soon as you feel happy you will most likely declare to yourself I am happy. But there is a major difference in saying I am happy to try and convince yourself that you are happy, while in actuality you are feeling angry, compared to actually feeling happy and making a declaration of, "I am happy." This seems like such an easy principle to see, but when it comes to growing our faith, most people seem to do it the incorrect way.

Without the acknowledgement of God's love, in combination with your belief in Him, nothing will be transformed in your life. Trust and belief in God is not a one way street. Your role to play in the part is limiting your doubt/unbelief. The Bible mentions that faith the size of a mustard seed is enough to do supernatural things. The majority of the time the problem we have today in the body of Christ is not a problem with our faith, or with our believing, but it has to do with our unbelief. It has to do with our doubt. The major contributor to the increase in doubt that I see in most Christians is the doubt that stems from the unresolved painful wounds that they carry from a hurtful and traumatic experience.

Any unresolved pain, hurt, and wounds that we carry inside of our subconscious mind, are going to automatically cause us to hold doubt. So no matter how hard we try and believe God for whatever it is we are praying for, we are not going to be able to receive it until we get rid of the doubt. We are not going to be able to get rid of the doubt caused by pain and hurt, until we get rid of the pain and hurt. We are not going to be able to get rid of the pain and hurt, until we fully forgive and heal from the situation. We are not going to be able to fully forgive and heal from the situation, until justice has been met regarding the wrongful and unjust acts that have been committed against us. I don't know of any other way, except through Jesus, as to how we are going to get justice from the uneven and unfair acts committed against us. Letting Him pay for the injustice, and take the iniquities onto His body that He has already paid for, is the only way I know of to become fully healed. In other words, admitting that Jesus' body was indeed bruised for our iniquities is the only way I know that will work. There is a reason Jesus said, "I am the way and the truth and the life."[10]

This is a major strategy that the enemy has been using against the body of Christ. He has been tearing people down from what has happened to them in their past. One of the enemy's primary goals is to get people to take their focus off of Jesus. He knows that if he is able to take people's focus off of Jesus, they will not be able to receive from God future blessings. Do you see what the enemy is doing? Can you see his strategy? He is trying to keep you focused on the times that you feel God let you down. He is trying to keep you constantly focused on your hurt, and the times when you were let down, so no matter how much you try to trust God to provide all His blessings in your future, it won't work. The unresolved pain a person holds speaks a message of, "God can't be trusted."

But understanding that Jesus was bruised on the cross and experienced our iniquities on His body tell us that God can indeed be trusted. This understanding enables you to focus on His love in the deeper areas that you could do before. I mentioned earlier that many Christians try and compartmentalize their faith with Jesus. They try and create faith in their conscious mind hoping that it will be strong enough to attract and receive the promises God has made in His word. It is true that what someone is focused on the most is exactly what they are going to attract. However, the subconscious mind holds a lot more power and weight than a person's conscious mind. The focus that is going inside of this area is going to do the majority of the attracting for the individual. We see the Bible mention this principle in Proverbs 4:23.

Keep thy heart with all diligence; for out of it are the issues of life.
Proverbs 4:23 (KJV)

The heart, which includes one's subconscious mind, is going to attract things to an individual. If your heart is full of anger, then you are going to experience a lot of angry situations in your life. If your heart is full of bitterness and unforgiveness, then you are going to experience a lot of hurtful situations in life. If you heart is full of love and joy, then you are going to attract a lot of contentment in life. So if you are not seeing the life you want on the outside, a change is needed on the inside. If you're focusing on hurt and pain on the inside, you won't be experiencing the life you desire on the outside.

I like to use the analogy of a flower that was created to spend the majority of its time in the sunlight. If you plant this flower in a garden, and allow it to be exposed to the right amount of sunlight, along with taking care of the other things it needs to grow, it will eventually bud in due time. But if you deprive the flower of light by building a metal enclosure all the way around it, it will eventually die, even if you still gave it all the other necessary things it needs to survive. I'm no gardening expert, but I do know flowers also need water, nutrients, and soil in order to grow, along with a few other things I am sure. So even if it got all the other things it needed to grow, but didn't get the sunlight, then the flower would eventually die. If the flower is focused on the sun in front of it, then it has a chance to live. The minute you build an enclosed fixture around it, to permanently block its focus from the sun, the flower will eventually die. The focus and positioning of the flower is a life or death issue. Likewise, our focus inside of ourselves is a life or death issue. If we focus our attention on hurt and pain, then our desires and dreams of what we want to achieve in life have no chance of manifesting. If we remove our focus from those things, through proper healing and forgiveness, we will find ourselves living the life we have always dreamed of.

The key lies in where our inner focus is. In order to receive from God, and to be transformed into Gods image, we need to focus on God's love with our whole being. We need to focus, meditate, and think about God's love with every fiber of our being, including our conscious and subconscious mind. The more we are focused on His love, the more we will begin to be transformed into His image, which ultimately means we will receive what we have trying to believe for. We see this idea in the book of 2 Corinthians.

And we all, who with unveiled faces contemplate the Lord's glory, are being transformed into his image with ever-increasing glory, which comes from the Lord, who is the Spirit.
2 Corinthians 3:18

When our hearts and subconscious minds are focused on God we are empowered to experience transformation. When our hearts are wounded and calloused, God cannot penetrate the blockage we keep up and take up residency in that critical area of our being. Most of us are only used to letting God take up residency in our conscious minds. We gladly give Him that area of our life, but our hearts seem to be a lot more difficult to relinquish. The problem is that if we keep trying to compartmentalize our faith it will short-circuit its power and effectiveness. We want to have it working in both our subconscious and conscious mind as it will strengthen our ability to believe, receive, and experience God's unconditional love.

As soon as God gave me a revelation that I could actually give my hurts to Him, I did it as fast as I could. Like I just mentioned, I saw the devastating effects of pain and hurt not only on myself, but also on the others close to me. I was so sick and tired of pain and hurt motivating me and running my life, robbing from me the things that I desired, and bringing me into a state of depression and shame. When you live that way long enough, it leaves a bitter taste in your mouth. I thank God for who He is, and I wake up each day with the fragrance of joy. If you are sick and tired of carrying the hurt and pain that has shackled you in your life, I encourage you to let it go. Forgive in the true sense of the word by understanding how Jesus has already paid for all those injustices you still carry. Justice came through Jesus Christ over two thousand years ago. If you have tried to forgive in the past, but never experienced full success, I suggest you add this missing piece.

I can testify that when I did so, my life was instantaneously transformed. I went from the incorrect way of renewing my mind (repeating scriptures over and over again, hoping one day I would believe them), to actually believing and experiencing the scriptures, having them bubble up from within me, which transformed my life.

So if you went through a breakup recently, or something else hurtful, you are free to continue on carrying that broken heart. God will never force you to give something up against your own free will; that is against His nature. If you choose to give up your broken heart, He will gladly take it and give you something indescribable in return. But the choice is yours. I respect whatever decision you make. I myself carried my broken heart for over ten years, so it would be very hypocritical of me to judge you for wanting to do the same. But you'll never find me walking down that pathway ever again. On that pathway I saw how much I destroyed myself, as well as others around me.

There's no part of me that desires to be in a relationship where I scheme up ways to get back at the girl that I am with. I apologize to my future wife, but if you do anything to upset me, or to make me angry, I am going to forgive you and love you back unconditionally. I'm sorry, but you're stuck with that. If you want someone who will pay you back hurt for hurt, then you better find someone else. Okay, before I get too sidetracked, let me finish up.

When you finally release and exchange your emotional wounds, your focus will move off of the pain, and onto Jesus' love. The Bible says in Isaiah 26:3 that *you will keep in perfect peace those whose minds are steadfast, because they trust in you.* Exchange with Jesus your emotional pain, so that your subconscious mind can be steadfast and focused on Him. Having our subconscious mind steadfast on Jesus will allow us to use our conscious mind to perform our daily tasks throughout the day. The beauty of this is that we never have to have our focus off of Jesus. The subconscious mind was meant to be a gift that we can use to live our life while never having to take our focus off of Jesus.

Let's take the example again of driving a car to see how powerful the subconscious mind truly is. When learning to drive a car, you need your full attention focused on what you are doing. You will be thinking about and telling yourself the steps that are needed to perform the task. As time goes by, you will become more comfortable performing the required tasks without having to be being consciously aware of what you are doing. I remember when I first learned how to drive a standard, I stalled so many times. I always had to pay close attention and tell my right hand to shift after my left foot pushed in the clutch. I had to pay even closer attention to that when I found myself on those dreaded hills. But over the course of time, and after doing it so much, I can now completely focus on the road ahead, without having to consciously think about what my right hand and left foot are doing. My subconscious is now totally aware of what needs to be done, and it takes over and performs the tasks for me, so I can focus on the road. This automatic performance is one of the functioning roles of the subconscious.

In the same manner, we want to fix our subconscious mind on Jesus, so we can go about our day without having to take our attention off of Jesus. Jesus knows we have lives to live, relationships to keep, and jobs to go to. Many people get stuck feeling pressured to have to compartmentalize their time with God and their regular life. This is never how God intended it to be, he gave us a subconscious mind for a reason, so that our focus can be on Him 24/7. It's always good to take time to bring your conscious mind into alignment with your inner focus; I'm not suggesting you never do that. I'm just saying don't settle for trying to have a relationship with God in only your conscious mind, while your subconscious mind remains wounded. Most people go through phases of telling themselves that they will spend more time praying, or reading their Bible. Then they get busy with work, friends, or life in general, and that falls on the back burner. When they start realizing their life is heading in a direction that they don't like, they try and go back to spending more time with Jesus again. Our relationship with Him doesn't need to be something that has to come and go.

I believe that once your focus is fully on Jesus, you will begin to see the supernatural in your life. We can't have our focus fully on Jesus when our subconscious mind is focused on pain and hurt. We need to let that go through what I discussed in the book, so we never have to take our spiritual eyes off of Him. When we can train ourselves to do this, I believe the supernatural has no choice but to show up. Then one day we will look at our lives and realize they have been transformed. We see this illustration of focus many times throughout the Bible. One of my favorite stories to exemplify this point is found in Mathew 14:22-33. In this passage we learn about the miracle of Jesus walking on the water. More specifically, in Mathew 14:28-30, we see Peter's experience of walking on water.

"Lord, if it's you," Peter replied, "tell me to come to you on the water."

"Come," he said.

Then Peter got down out of the boat, walked on the water and came toward Jesus. But when he saw the wind, he was afraid and, beginning to sink, cried out, "Lord, save me!"
Mathew 14:28-30

From these verses we see that Peter steps out of the boat, walks on top of the water, and makes his way to Jesus. The Bible does not account for how many steps Peter took on top of the water, but it does bring our attention to an important principle. That is, that as long as Peter kept his full focus and attention on Jesus, he was able to perform the supernatural. The minute Peter focused part of his attention on the wind, he became afraid, and He started to sink. The same thing goes for us in our lives. The minute we hold fear, or hurt, in our hearts and subconscious mind, it takes away our ability to fully focus on Jesus. As a result, our belief in Him, and our ability to walk in the supernatural, becomes hindered. When we decide to let go of the pain and hurt in our hearts and subconscious mind, we will be enabled to transform our lives supernaturally.

If you desire a transformed life in any area that you have been hoping for and praying for, I am sorry to burst your bubble, but it will be impossible to achieve if you hold onto hurt, pain, and unforgiveness, as these things will increase unbelief. It is against human nature to experience pain and hurt, and keep on growing your trust and belief. That is, without Jesus it is impossible! But with Him, all things are possible![11] The fact that He paved the way for you to exchange your hurts and pains in exchange for His love grows our belief and decreases our unbelief. The exact recipe we need to strengthen and further our relationship with God.

We learned earlier that forgiveness will need justice in order to be complete. Unless we understand that justice has been served on Jesus' body, that He died for our iniquities, I do not know where else it can come from. If we have been hurt and unjustly wronged, that is a big deal. For some reason I feel Christians don't give that enough attention. We are always focusing on our sins, and how we wronged ourselves and other people. We are always focusing on Jesus for the exchange and forgiveness of those things. But we never give much attention to focusing on the times where we have been completely and utterly wronged. The truth is, if something wrong happened to you, something that you didn't deserve, it actually happened and occurred. It is impossible to just ignore that it happened, to sweep it under the rug, and to act like it's no big deal. If it was not a big deal, then Jesus would not have died on the cross for it. God knew beforehand how big of a deal it was, and He made sure that Jesus paid for it. Sins are a big deal, and we see how important they are to God by looking at the brutality that Jesus went through on the cross to save us from them. To God, iniquities are also a big deal, and we see that again by looking at Jesus dying on the cross, and all the brutality that He took to save us from them as well. It's time we as Christians stop focusing solely on God taking away our sins alone. It's time we start glorifying God for all that He has paid for and done.

I don't know any other way to complete and full healing through forgiveness, then through Him. All other forms of forgiveness miss the piece about justice. Only Jesus offers forgiveness with justice included. Without the missing piece about justice, then forgiveness is incomplete. And from chapter 1, we already learned about the dangers of being incomplete. The only other way I know to gain justice is through the avenue of revenge. But in that avenue, you don't really gain true justice, plus you lose out on forgiveness. Only Jesus offers forgiveness and justice together. To Jesus, that is exactly what true forgiveness is. Any other form of forgiveness is an imitation.

I feel as a body of Christ, we have been missing this piece about true forgiveness for a long time. We have been trying to forgive ourselves, and accept ourselves, in our own strength. We have also been trying to believe God for things in our lives, things that we see promised to His children in the Bible, but are always left wondering when they will come. People tell us in church, that if we just keep believing long enough, if we just stay constant and not waver, that we will receive them. Technically, that is true. But the practical ways of believing, of staying consistent, and of not wavering that we have been using in the past, are not successfully working. There is a stereotype in the church that people fall into. This stereotype is that people think and believe they can create the necessary levels of faith, in their conscious mind alone. But like we have seen earlier, if the subconscious mind feels differently it will override all the believing that a person can muster up.

I am not aware of any other way to meet the requirements of justice and forgiveness than through Jesus Christ. This justice will help us answer the doubting based question of understand where God was during our painful experiences. We know exactly where He was! He was on the cross, experiencing the exact pain and trauma that you felt. So if you have ever been cheated on, He was on the cross going through the exact painful experiences in His soul that you experienced. All the tears, sadness, and betrayal which you felt from the person that cheated on you, He also chose to experience. If a man named John cheated on you, then Jesus knows exactly what it is like to be cheated on by John. If a girl named Ann cheated on you, then He knows exactly what it is like to be cheated on by Ann. No matter the situation, no matter the circumstance, no matter the unique experiences, Jesus knows them all, and He decided to feel them all in His body. If you were raped, or abused, He was on the cross going through those exact painful experiences in His soul that you experienced. If you were abandoned, gone through a divorce or breakup, lost a loved one, whatever the case may be, He knows exactly what it is like to go through exactly what you went through.

I could go on and on with a list of traumatic experiences, but if I did that, I am sure my book would never end. I am sure there are many people in the world who have been unjustly wronged for no reason, if not every single person living. But the good news is that Jesus wanted you to have a way to overcome it, and to be able to live life to the fullest. He wanted to prove to you that He still accepts you, and that He loves you unconditionally, no matter what the injustice may be. He came to take it all on, so He could demonstrate to you that you are not damaged goods, but that you are His sons and daughters. You are all princes and princesses. I don't know any other greater love than that. He didn't just experience pain and hurt in general, but as we see in the Bible, He was bruised for our iniquities. Not just an overall everyone's iniquities, but OUR iniquities! He felt all the unique, personalized, and individualized wounds. That's a lot of painful experiences to feel. The world is a big place. There are a lot of painful stories. But Jesus didn't care, in fact He insisted on experiencing it. Plus, like I mentioned earlier, He had the chance to take wine mixed with gall, so that the pain He felt would subside, but He willingly chose not to for our sake.

What a loving father, what a loving God. It is time we as Christians stop shortchanging what Jesus accomplished on the cross. Not only did He die for our sins, but He was also bruised for our iniquities. I have no idea why both of these aren't celebrated and worshiped when we go to church. We tend to only focus on the forgiveness of sins the majority of the time. I was even at a service one time where the verse in Romans 4:7 was used to make a point.

Saying, Blessed are they whose iniquities are forgiven, and whose sins are covered.
Romans 4:7 (KJV)

The church read the verse, and then the point was made about how great it is that Jesus died to cover our sins. Then the sermon kept on going as if the iniquities part had no value. It's time we all give credit to where credit is due. It's time we start praising God for everything Jesus did on the cross, not just part of it. After all, we should know by now the dangers of being incomplete. In this case, the danger results in a whole bunch of Christians receiving God's forgiveness of sins, but living their life never knowing that His love for them is so much deeper than just that act alone. He doesn't just love you, accept you, and forgive you for what you have done wrong; He also loves you, and accepts you, even with all the wrongful and shameful acts committed against you. If we have been abused, abandoned, divorced, whatever the case may be, it's time we stop believing the shameful lie that we are damaged goods. The truth is you're the apple of God's eye! You're not a mistake. He smiles every time the thought of you crosses His mind, which is quite a few times according to the Bible. What a glorious gospel.

For I am not ashamed of the gospel, because it is the power of God that brings salvation to everyone who believes: first to the Jew, then to the Gentile.
Romans 1:16

The gospel is the power of God, and will bring salvation to everyone who believes. We read and see that if we can believe, then we will experience salvation and the power of God. There are numerous scriptures that talk about God's promises, and that if a person believes them, they will attain, or receive, that promise. I've gone to many churches, many great ones, but when it comes to how to practically believe, I've never learned how to do it. This to me seems very odd. Shouldn't I leave church feeling I know exactly what to practically do! Like I mentioned earlier in this book, when it came to renewing my mind, people would always tell me the importance of actually renewing my mind, but when it came to how I could practically do it, the advice I got was not complete enough to get the job done. It was not enough to get the transformation that I desired.

The same thing goes for the statement, "God loves you." I have gone to so many churches that tell you that God does indeed love you. They spend time teaching the congregation about how to love people, telling you how to love someone back if they hurt you or make you feel angry. To me this process of learning seems very incomplete. Knowing what to do, and actually being able to successfully execute and do it, are two completely different things. I could take you out for coffee and tell you how to play tennis. I could bring my laptop along and show you all the ways to swing your arm properly for each tennis stroke there is. But wouldn't it make more sense going to the tennis court and have you experience what I am teaching you also? The same thing goes for what we teach in church. It's no good if we teach people what to do but never show them how to do it, knowing what to do in a situation pales in comparison to actually being able to successfully do it. We need to teach people that God loves them by showing them that God loves them, not just by simply saying it.

So how do we show people that God loves them? The first thing we need to do is become more loving ourselves. We need to become loving in nature. We need the love of Jesus to move into every area of our being. After He has moved into every area of our being, people will have no choice but to feel His love every time they come into contact with us.

MOVING JESUS INTO OUR HEARTS

I mentioned earlier that we as a body of Christ have made the mistake of compartmentalizing our relationship with God. Another area we make the mistake of compartmentalization can be seen in the different parts we allow Jesus access to. When we invite Jesus into our lives, He comes to reside in our spirit. For most people, this is where Jesus stays. He often never makes His way into any other parts of our being. But what good does Jesus do living in our spirits, but never making His way into our hearts, our minds, and our souls? People we interact with will be interacting with our hearts, our minds, and our souls. If Jesus is not welcomed into these areas of our lives, then the people we interact with will never experience the type of love that only Jesus can offer.

When we become a Christian, only our spirit gets renewed. Jesus moving from our spirit into our heart, mind, and soul, becomes our responsibility. However, most of us never give Him permission to do so. Jesus can't move into one's heart, one's mind, and one's soul, until they invite Him in. Before we became Christians, Jesus' gift of the forgiveness of sins was available to us at any time. But Jesus couldn't give us the gift of forgiveness against our free will; that would be against His nature. We first need to recognize that we are sinful and that we need forgiveness. It wouldn't be possible to receive forgiveness if you never knew you needed it. In other words, it's impossible to receive something that you don't believe you need. The same principle applies when it comes to our mind and the unresolved pain we keep inside of there.

After we invite Jesus into our lives, the most important thing we can do next is to renew our mind. As soon as we become a Christian we have Jesus living on the inside of us. But we still possess the same mind that is accustomed to living the way it did before we became Christians. That is why renewing of the mind is so vital. I like to use the analogy of driving a different car. You may know what I am talking about here. Let's imagine you borrow, buy, or rent a different car than the one you are accustomed to driving. There is going to be different functions inside of that car. The lever for the windshield wipers may be on the opposite side. The gas cap may be on the different side. The car may even be standard or automatic, and this may be opposite to what you are accustomed to with your old car. As you drive and perform different tasks you will notice the differences in the car. Your mind has been programmed to the car you are used to driving. So if the gas tank is on the left in your old car, but in the new car it is on the right, you will find yourself pulling up to the pump on the wrong side the first few times. This is because your mind has been ingrained with all the properties of your old car. It takes time changing these habits to fit the new car you find yourself driving. The same thing goes for renewing our mind when it comes to our new life with Jesus. All the newness that Jesus offers us will be quite different than what we are used to from our life lived without Him as our Lord and Savior. Hence, this is why renewing our minds is so important.

Many of us have Jesus living inside of our spirits, but inside of our hearts, our mind, and our souls, we have pain residing. Jesus living in our spirit, but not in our mind, is not going to be beneficial for us. Jesus residing in certain parts of our being is not something we want to compartmentalize. We want Jesus living inside of us in every possible area. As we saw earlier, failure to do so will lead to double-mindedness. Double-mindedness will lead to doubt. And doubt will lead to not being able to receive God's wonderful promises.

Allowing Jesus to move from our spirit into our mind is something we are responsible for. When we have pain and hurt residing inside of our mind, it is up to us to release that to Jesus. If we don't, we will keep on experiencing life the same way we did before we became Christians. Like I have repeated throughout this book, renewing one's mind includes the renewal of both thoughts and emotions, as the mind is the area where unresolved emotions are stored. Our heart, mind, and soul are all connected. If I use these words interchangeably, know that I am referring to one's emotional state that is found in one's mind. Each of these areas is going to have painful experiences that have been built up over the course of our lives, and these experiences will have caused serious wounds. Unless of course you have never been hurt before in this life, which in that cases you have nothing to sweat. But I'll be very surprised if that is the case. All of the wounds we have will need the love of Jesus to enter in before we can experience restoration and the necessary healing. If we don't decide to give Jesus the wounds that reside inside of our mind, then we will live life as if we weren't saved in the first place. We will be still saved in our spirit, but we will never be able to manifest and experience any of God's promises that are rightfully ours.

What good is it to be a Christian and live a life where we don't ever see any fruit of that decision? We are supposed to be blessed and experiencing love, joy, and peace. What good is it to experience love, joy, and peace inside of our spirit, but never feel those fruits inside of our hearts, minds, and souls? This inevitably happens to all of us when we don't allow Jesus to move into the entire area of our hearts. We can't keep going on giving Jesus parts of our hearts, while trying to keep from Him the parts of our hearts that we believe are damaged and in pain. Jesus is a healer, and if we don't give Him access to our pains, how can He come in and heal them? Many of us have been holding onto unresolved pain inside of our minds and it has been robbing us of our joy. Not only does it rob us from parts of God's love, but it also robs other people from experiencing the fullness of God's love.

The people we interact with here on earth will be interacting with our hearts, our minds, and our souls. Especially our spouse, who is our deepest relationship we experience outside of our relationship with God. He or she will be interacting with those areas the most. If we have not let the love of God come into the entirety of our hearts, our minds, and our souls, then others around us will be experiencing a mixture of God's love and our pain. In the areas of our heart that we have given to Jesus, they will taste His love, but in the areas we keep unresolved pain, they will taste anything but the love of God.

We as a church have made the mistake of compartmentalizing our relationship with God. If we have been wounded in the past and have yet to let Jesus come into those given areas, then even though Jesus lives in our spirit, the people in close contact with us will never ever experience Him. The Bible tells us in Philippians 2:12 to *work out our own salvation.* Part of this process includes making room in the areas of our life that Jesus has not moved into yet. This is why the Bible is clear when it say in Romans 12:2 to *be transformed by the renewing of our minds.* Once we have more and more parts of our mind renewed, it creates more and more room for Jesus to take up residency inside of us. We need to understand that this choice is something that we are responsible for. This is something that falls on our side of the equation.

I mentioned before that the problem most people have when it comes to their relationship with God is that they are in the way. Our unresolved pain is something that clearly gets in God's way. His ability to bless us is severely hindered when we choose to continually carry unresolved pain. There is nothing wrong with the law of healing that is found in the Bible. We see the Bible mention numerous times that Jesus healed multitudes of people. The ability of Jesus healing people like that today still exists. I believe one of the main reasons we don't see much of His healing power is because we have lost the understanding of how to receive. Receiving requires us to believe and not doubt. It's this ability to not doubt that I see so many people struggle with. When one understands the relationship between unresolved pain and how it relates to doubt, it's not hard to see why we haven't seen much of God's power in our lives. It's time we start letting Jesus have full access to our lives. It's not good keeping certain part of our lives from Him.

Giving up our wounds and placing them on Jesus' body empowers Jesus to then come into those areas and take up residency. Once He is in there you will feel brand new. The Bible teaches us that you will be a new creation. You will feel so new that the painful hurtful experiences that you once held inside of there will feel like they are a thing of the past. Once this process is complete, congratulations, you have successfully achieved transformation. Remember what the definition of transformation is from chapter 2. Transformation means to make a thorough or dramatic change in the form, appearance, or character of something, usually implying for the better. Is not Jesus coming into an area that was once wounded and experiencing pain, but is now a place where you are experiencing joy, love, completeness, and healing, sound like transformation? That's exactly what it sounds like to me.

Most people are familiar with transforming their thoughts. If you have a negative, hurtful, and unwanted thought, you replace that thought with a thought that is positive, comforting, and desirable. Most people are not as familiar though with transforming their emotions. However the process is not that different. If you have a negative, hurtful, and unwanted emotion, you replace that emotion with an emotion that is positive, comforting, and desirable. The only difference is that the way you actually do it is going to be a little bit different. However, after reading the book, hopefully it is not complicated anymore.

Like I said earlier, for some reason many people use the process that works for renewing their thoughts and they try to make it work for renewing their emotions. To me this is a very foolish thing to do. One of the variables has changed it the problem. One problem deals with thoughts, the other deals with emotions. The same process won't work when new variables are introduced.

If you go inside your car and turn the key, it will start, and you can drive it to wherever your heart desires. But if I go inside of your car and pop the hood and proceed to take out the engine, when you come to start your car it is not going to start. You will need a different process since a variable has changed. The old process will no longer satisfy the function of the car getting you to your desired destination. A new process could of course be cutting a hole in the bottom of your car, and you then trying to pull a Fred Flintstone. (Sorry if I outdated some of you with that reference). A more logical option would be to put the engine back in, and then turn your key to start your car. Just because a process worked in one set of circumstances, it does not mean it will work if the circumstances change. I see a lot of people in the body of Christ who do not renew their emotions, and they expect that the process that worked for them when they renewed their thoughts, will also work for them when they renew their emotions. But after reading this book, that unawareness should no longer be an issue.

THE FRUIT OF LOVE

We can carry our pain, hurt, and shame for our entire life if we choose to, Jesus will never overstep our free will and force healing, value, love, and wholeness onto us. If we want to keep our pains, our hurts, and our wounds, we are completely free to do so. But when we choose to carry them, Jesus is not allowed to give us the gifts of healing, joy, and acceptance in that area. The only time He becomes empowered to be able to give us those wonderful emotions is when we choose that we want them. As soon as we choose we want those things, the process is very similar to the way we give Him our sins. We acknowledge that He was bruised for the unjust acts that we have experienced, we ask Him to take them, He takes them, and in return He gives you a piece of Himself. Once that piece of Him lives in the area that the pain was living in, you will feel His loving nature living in there, instead of the pain that you felt before.

The Bible tells us in 1 John 4:8 that *God is love*. God's nature is love. The Greek word for love here is agape. This means an unconditional form of love that is greater in power than the typical form of love that people are used to in the world. It is this love that can influence the people we interact with in this world. It is impossible to produce this kind of love in our own strength. It's against our human nature. If we could actually produce this kind of love on our own, we wouldn't have the need for a Lord and Savior. It's time we as a church learn to become more loving natured in all the areas of our being. This is just as important to learn as compared to knowing what to do in given situations. I find as a church we spend too much time trying to know what to do, and how to behave. If we spend more time learning how to transform more areas of our life to look like Christ, we will automatically respond and behave the proper way. The problem that I see many Christians have is they know what they should do, but they don't know how to actually live it out. Most Christians know that when their spouse makes them angry, and hurts their feelings, that they should forgive them and show them back love. Christians aren't unaware of this principle that will help their marriage. But many of them are unaware of how to actually forgive their spouse, and how to show them love when they face that exact scenario. What good is knowing what to do, but not being able to execute it? Both are essential!

The only way in this scenario to actually be able to forgive their spouse, and to keep showing them love, is if they possess God's nature in the area that is being pressured. If I put pressure on lemons, hence I squeeze them, lemon juice is going to come out. When pressure is applied to something, what is inside is going to come out. Likewise, when we find ourselves in difficult situations, what we are made of is going to come out.

In this situation with our spouse, we may be Christians and have Jesus living inside of our spirit, but if the argument is putting pressure on our hearts, then if we have not let Jesus come into that area of our hearts, His nature won't be squeezed out. The most important thing we can do as Christians is to renew our minds. True renewing of the mind is taking Jesus from our spirit, and giving Him permission to come and live inside of our heart, mind, and soul. That way when we experience pressures, Jesus effortlessly and automatically comes out. Once Jesus comes out of us under pressure type situations, it grows our confidence and trust in Him. It also allows other people who may have never tasted Jesus' love before, to experience it through you. The whole point of being a Christian in the first place is so that you can carry God and demonstrate and show His love to others. There is a reason the Bible tells us that our bodies are temples. The living God resides inside of us. When people are around us, they should feel like they have been walking with God once they leave.

The fruits of the Spirit talked about in Galatians chapter 5:22-23 are: *love, joy, peace, patience, kindness, goodness, faithfulness, gentleness, self-control.* (ESV) There is a reason they are called the fruits of the Spirit! That is because the Holy Spirit is the only One who will be able to produce them. If you could produce them in your own strength, you wouldn't need the help of the Holy Spirit. There is no use teaching people how to be joyful, loving, kind, and self controlled, without teaching them how to allow the Holy Spirit to come and take up residency in their life. Loving your spouse unconditionally, even when they hurt you, is quite easy when the Holy Spirit resides inside of your heart, mind, and soul. It's time we start giving permission to Jesus to have full access to our lives. Without full access, we will never experience full transformation.

In order to experience complete healing and transformation to take place in your life, you need to see and understand His justice for what happened to you in the past. Once you recognize this you will feel justified. You need to feel fully justified before you can fully forgive. You need to fully forgive before you can have the confidence to allow yourself to be vulnerable with God. Finally, you need to be able to be vulnerable with God before you can be vulnerable with other people again. *If you are not able to be vulnerable, you will not be able to experience love at a deeper level.* Once you give Jesus your iniquities, you will experience true forgiveness. Once you make this exchange, Jesus can then come and live in the area where the pain was. You releasing the pain will make space for Him to be able to live. There is no room for Him to live in your heart, mind, and soul when unresolved pain takes up the space. You making room, by releasing the pain, is what God is waiting for. Once you make the room and God moves in, you will feel more loved by God, and He will continue to show you more and more of His love for you, which will just keep on growing your belief and trust in Him. Once you reach this point of fully trusting and believing in Him, you will be able to receive from Him the things you have been praying for. Then you will see your life flowing with the things that you need, want, and desire in your future.

I trust you can now see how believing practically works, and how you can grow your trust and belief. This area of Jesus taking on our iniquities is something I've never heard at church. But it's right there in the Bible! It's time we know that Jesus did this, and start focusing on it more. If we don't grow in our understanding of who Jesus is, we will never grow our trust. Think about it, before you were a Christian, and understood that Jesus paid for your sins, you didn't have any trust in Him. Once you realized He did this, you started to trust Him and a new relationship was born. Knowing Jesus more increases our trust! It's time we acknowledge the fact that Jesus died for our iniquities.

IF YOU ARE NOT ABLE TO BE *VULNERABLE,* YOU WILL NOT BE ABLE TO EXPERIENCE LOVE AT A DEEPER LEVEL

I'll try one more relationship analogy to try and drive this point home. I don't know why I love these relationship analogies so much, maybe it's just the way my mind works. I hope it will help you understand it more clearly also. Not focusing on all that Jesus died and paid for is like a husband buying flowers for his wife on her wedding day. That becomes all she focuses on; paying no attention to all the loving things he does for her after. It is true that the husband buying his wife flowers is very loving. But for her to only focus on this one loving act for the rest of her life would be silly. Imagine he keeps buying her flowers, taking her on trips, and constantly helping out around the house. But for some reason all she sees and focuses on is the fact the he bought her flowers on their wedding day. Wouldn't this be silly! Wouldn't it be more powerful if she focused on all the loving actions he did. Wouldn't she feel a deeper sense of love from her husband if she focused on the fact that he bought her flowers on their wedding day, plus every other loving act that he has done. Of course it would. Likewise, it's time we do the same thing with Jesus as well. We have spent so much time focusing on Him dying for our sins. Why don't we focus on that, plus the fact that He was bruised for our iniquities! Won't this make us feel an even deeper sense of love towards our Savior! Won't this automatically grow our trust in Him! Of course it will. When we start seeing Him dying for our sins and our iniquities, it will make us feel more loved and accepted, which in turn makes us feel more free to be who we truly are.

When we are hurt and wounded, one of the main things we want to know and feel is that we are not alone; knowing that we are known, and knowing that we are not alone, is one of the deepest human needs. Everybody has a longing for this deep within them. Jesus taking on all the injustices, and wrongs done to us, provides a way for that longing to be fulfilled. Jesus Himself, who was God in the flesh, didn't have to come to feel and experience all the temptations, hurts, pains, and wounds that human beings can feel and experience. But He wanted to demonstrate His unconditional love for us. He decided to come down from heaven, where He had everything going for Him, and where He experienced no pain. He decided to come to earth to experience every single kind of pain that there is all in order to be able to relate to us, and to be able to have a relationship with us. I don't know of any other entity that loves me that much, and that would do all of that for me. That kind of love I only find in Him. To know that God Himself not only knows me, but that He loves me unconditionally, that leaves me feeling valuable, worthy, and honored. And when I say unconditionally, I mean unconditionally. Not like how certain religious folks see unconditionally. I mean, the fact that God loves me so much, even with all of the hurtful things I have done to myself and others in the past, plus all the brokenness, pain, and hurt I have tasted from other people on this earth, is quite mind blowing. Those two things in combination, not one alone without the other, make us feel loved, and it gives us a peace that transcends all understanding.

When it comes to valuing yourself for who you are, that part is going to need to be believed. One can't just say I'm valued, keep repeating it to themselves, and expect it to become true. You actually treating yourself as someone who is valued will never come to be until you actually believe it. Knowing Jesus took on your iniquities will help you believe it, because through it He shows you just how valuable you are to Him. It shows you how valuable you are in His eyes. He didn't have to come and take it on His body, but He wanted to, He chose to, and through this choice, He shows you how valuable you truly are. Without that understanding, belief, and revelation, you will not treat yourself as valuable. If you don't value yourself, you can't expect others to either. It's time we start seeing how precious we truly are. It's time to start treating ourselves, and loving ourselves, in a way which lines up to that truth. It's time we start loving other people that exact same way. This will all happen when we stop feeling inadequate before God. It's time we stop viewing ourselves as damaged goods, as being inadequate, and as having too much baggage. Those are all lies from the enemy. We are accepted unconditionally. We belong to God!

Drug addict, abuse victim, outcast, that is not what God sees. He chose to take those emotions, those pains, and those labels on His own body, so that He could view you as perfect. No matter what you have experienced in life, God sees you as someone far beyond what words can describe. That's why He went to the cross so that He could prove to you how deeply He desires a relationship with you. That way He can show you, and also tell you, just how much love He has for you, as you walk hand in hand through life. Because after all, a relationship and love are abstract things, He can't relay them to you in any other way.

The most common stereotype I see Christian people believing is that they need to change in order for God to accept them. We don't need to change for God to accept us. We just need to see how much God loves us first, and after we taste that, transformation becomes something that is inevitable. It's time we start focusing on His love that He demonstrated to us through the fact that He was bruised for our iniquities. Just like how a rose bush is positioned and focused towards the sun, and will eventually transform and bud beautiful roses. It's time we focus our subconscious mind, and any pain that exists in there, towards the Son of God; so that our lives can be transformed, and we can begin to bud the things that God has always wanted us to have.

His unconditional love gave me the ability to rise up out of addictions, it empowered me to truly love myself and others, and it gave me this new found ability to take all of my pains, hurts, wounds, and disappointments, and turn them into love. You can ask anyone who knew me in the past, if you made me angry, or hurt me, then you better be expecting that same thing coming right back at you. I no longer need to take hurt and give hurt. I can now take hurt and wrong doing coming my way, give it to Jesus ,thanks to the fact that He bore all my iniquities, receive His love in exchange for my gift of pain to Him, and keep on loving myself, as well as the person who wronged me. I trust and believe that you have the same ability to exchange this with Jesus as well. Unless of course, you want to keep on carrying the hurts and pains caused to you in your past. Since Jesus loves you so much, He will actually respect your free will decision to keep on carrying them. But if you ask me, there's no point of Him carrying my hurts, as well as me. That's a waiting out game that you will never win. Because never ever, will Jesus change the fact of His decision to experience the hurtful pain that you experienced. It's impossible, as He did it over two thousand years ago on the cross. I'm sorry, but you're stuck with the fact that Jesus will always love you, and will always accept you unconditionally. That is impossible to change. But you're free to choose to not accept it.

Have you ever heard the phrase, *it's not what you say, but how you say it*? The reason for this is because there is energy and life behind words. When we are communicating with people we listen to this energy more than we do the actual words. After all, the function of words is to try and convey this energy to another. This same principle applies when we are talking to ourselves. True positive thinking, or renewing of the mind, does not occur with thoughts alone. It occurs with the entirety of the mind. In order to renew our minds properly, we are going to need Jesus. We are going to need to give Him our emotions, our hurts, and our wounds, before we can experience the transformed life that we desire.

Jesus tells us in Mark 12:30 to *love the Lord your God with all your heart and with all your soul and with all your mind and with all your strength.* It's time we as a body of Christ stop loving God with parts of our heart, parts of our soul, and parts of our mind, and parts of our strength. It's time we start loving God fully with all of those things. If we have hurt and pain inside of us, we can't fully love God by holding those things back from Him. Think about it, if you have children, or if you have a significant other, how would you feel if they only gave you what they thought were the perfect parts of them, and always kept you in the dark about the parts that were messy and hurtful inside of them? Wouldn't you feel closer, more intimate, and experience a deeper sense of love with them, if they were transparent with their entire self. The same thing goes with our relationship with Jesus. It's time we stop hiding and pretending that we don't have emotional pain inside of us. If we actually are wounded inside, it's not something we need to hide from Jesus. It's time we bring those things to light, and give Him what He has already rightfully paid for. It's time we stop robbing from Jesus the painful scars that we experienced in life, and give Him what He paid for. They were never meant for us to carry and keep inside. They were meant for us to give to Jesus in exchange for His love. We as Christians have no problem giving Him our sins in exchange for His love. It's time we become just as motivated to give Him the wrongs done to us, the injustices, the unfairness, and the unevenness. When we finally are able to accomplish this, the positive words we declare over ourselves will have energy and power behind them.

The Bible tells us in John 10:10 that *the thief comes only to steal and kill and destroy; I have come that they may have life, and have it to the full.* Our unresolved painful wounds are one way the enemy has been allowed to keep on robbing things from us in our lives. Jesus has already stripped all power and authority from Satan through what He did on the cross.[12] If we don't understand the part about Jesus dying on the cross for our iniquities, then we are giving power to Satan, who in actuality has no power. He can then come into our lives and have his way. But as soon as we as a body of Christ start acknowledging the fact that Jesus paid for our iniquities, that He paid the price for the wrongful acts done to us, we will undoubtedly feel more loved by Him. This new found love, wholeness, value, and acceptance we feel from God, will cause us to love Him all the more. It will help us see Him in a whole new light. And it will allow us to fully trust, believe, and rely on Him. Trusting, believing, and relying on God, is not something that we are required to come up with in our own strength. It is meant to be something that we receive from God, which then in turn transforms us.

This is how trust and belief is grown. It is not something that we need to manufacture on our own. The more we see, understand, and focus on just how much God loves us, it will cause our trust and belief to grow automatically. When we see His love for us, His acceptance of us even with our hurts, and the fact that He would go as far as to feel them Himself to prove how much He loves us, then believing isn't something we need to muster up, or to create, it becomes a reflex to understanding all that He has done. If you have been living your life lately trying to create trust in God in order to receive something from Him, but having no success, I suggest you start changing your procedure and start focusing more on God's love for you. Once you do this, you will see your trust and belief in Him grow effortlessly. Before you know it, you will be manifesting and walking in the promises of God, the very ones that you have been trying to attain for so long. Once you finally get there, you will find yourself glorifying and worshiping God like you never have before.

RESTORATION

CHAPTER 8

In closing, if we look back on how we became Christians in the first place, we will see that we came to an understanding, a revelation, of the fact that Jesus died for our sins. That kind and loving act shifted our hearts. Tasting His great love caused us to repent from our sins. Tasting His love first is what changes us. Tasting His love first is what transforms us. That is why everything from God can only be received. He gives us gifts, gifts that transform us. Mercy can't be mercy, and grace can't be grace, if it is not a gift. They need to come first and transform us, not the other way around. If we try to do it the other way around, we are acting incomplete.

If the code to a safe is 1-2-3-4-5, the safe will not open if you type in 5-4-3-2-1. That is not precise, that is not complete. You have the exact same numbers, but they are in the wrong order. Likewise, when it comes to receiving from God, the proper order is essential if we want to unlock our hearts, to unlock our potential, and to unlock the life that we have always longed for, dreamed of, and desired. We will not taste and experience it if we don't first fully understand God's love for us. Jesus died for our sins, and when we hear that at church, we never forget that fact. It makes us feel truly loved. It's time we as a church keep on remembering this great act, and also start remembering and focusing on the fact that Jesus also died for our iniquities. It is foolish to focus on the one, without focusing on the other. If you're a parent of three, it's not very loving of you to focus on one child, and forget about the other two. If you're in a relationship, it's foolish to focus on your first date over and over again, while paying no attention to the other loving dates and experiences together. It's time we as a body of Christ start doing the same with our loving Lord and Savior Jesus Christ.

We as a church have been using a Band-Aid solution when it comes to how we have been believing. It's time we become aware that the way we have been believing is not working. We need to become aware that we have swept this issue under the rug for so long. We preach great sermons, we spend lots of time going to church, and many of us are dedicated to reading our Bibles, but I have yet to find a church to properly show its followers how to practically believe. There's no use in continuing this process while failing to tell people how to practically do what's preached. What good is telling people about Jesus while failing to show them who Jesus is! What good is telling people they can transform their lives, find peace, and taste Jesus' love, but never telling them how to do that? I go to so many churches who talk about what Jesus can offer people, but they never give them any practical ways of how they can get there. What good is an explanation without direction? What good is knowledge without wisdom? What good is information without revelation? Both need to go hand in hand if they are going to benefit and bless a person. Telling a person they will experience an amazing life if they believe in the Bible, but never showing them how to believe, does not do much to enhance one's life. It's time we as a body of Christ start teaching and enabling others. Failure to do so will keep us regarded as another powerless religion, something Christianity was never meant to be.

The main life giving source is missed when we constantly study the scriptures to train ourselves to respond a certain way. I wrote this book because I see so many churches doing this when it comes to their understanding regarding renewing one's mind. People trying to watch what they say because they know words have power. People trying to train themselves to always respond and declare positive things like, "God loves me." They spend so much time watching what they say, and what is going through their thoughts, all because they are trying to make sure they never think or say anything negative. This is a Band-Aid solution when it comes to renewing one's mind. This process will work when one's thoughts are the only thing that needs renewing. But the majority of the time I see people using this technique to mask the pain that they feel deep inside. Most people are ignorant to the fact that they are trying to renew negative emotions with positive thoughts. They mistakenly perceive negative emotions for positive

thoughts. They wonder why they hear so many negative things, and their solution to fix the problem is repeating positive things. This misunderstanding leads a person into a state of denial. Most of the time people don't feel God's full love for them, so they end up trying to change that feeling by repeating a statement that is truthful. But a truthful statement has no power to transform a person unless it is believed.
An emotion is impossible to change without experiencing another emotion in its place. The emotion of shame can't be shed by declaring, "I am accepted." The emotion of shame needs to be exchanged for the emotion of acceptance, then when the emotion of acceptance becomes a feeling that an individual experiences, they will believe and feel the feeling of acceptance.

It is true that the name of Jesus has power. But the nature of Jesus has more power than His name alone. You can't be residing in something opposite of Jesus' nature and expect to use His name to take you out of where you are. If you are angry and holding onto strife and bitterness, you can't successfully declare, "I am happy in Jesus name." His name alone isn't what takes you out of anger, bitterness, and strife. His nature is what will take you out of those destructive things. You can't go through a divorce and declare, "In Jesus name I'm happy," and expect for happiness to result. You can't feel worthless and declare, "In Jesus name I'm amazing," and expect to feel whole. You need to understand the nature of Jesus and His name in order to be transformed. As soon as you experience God's true nature, you will believe it, and you will find yourself effortlessly transformed. Trying to do this process backwards will not work. The Bible tells us that out of the heart, the mouth speaks. So you need to change what's in your heart, not change the way you speak. When you change what's in your heart, you will automatically change the way you speak.

Experiencing your significant other loving you will increase your belief that they do indeed love you. Them saying they love you, but having their actions not match their words, is not going to make you feel loved by them. It is with the combination of words and actions that a person believes something to be true. Drop the experience and you won't comprehend the feeling of love.

It's time we as a body of Christ start teaching others the experience of God's love, instead of trying to brainwash people to believe what we believe. It doesn't take a rocket scientist to see that church attendance is dwindling worldwide. I believe one of the main reasons for this is because there are not too many churches modeling the fullness of Jesus' love. How do you expect other people to believe that Jesus loves them when they have never tasted or experienced that kind of love? How do you expect them to experience that kind of love if they aren't going to experience it through you?

Jesus Christ died so that He could come and reside in you. He wanted to live inside of you so that others would taste his presence every time they were around you. How do you expect to model this kind of unconditional love in your own strength? Most of us, if we get in a fight with our significant other, will respond back with anything but love. If we can't model Christ's love in our own relationships, how do we expect to demonstrate it to people we don't even know? If someone treats you with disrespect and shows you a lack of love, if you respond back the exact same way, how do you expect them to ever see God's love?

Think about this type of love in your relationship or marriage. If your significant other does something to hurt you, and you respond back with more hurt, how do you think they are going to respond back to you once things come full circle? If your significant other gets mad at you, and you respond back by getting mad at them, tell me how that breaks the vicious cycle of destruction? If you learn to meet pain, hurt, and disappointment with unconditional love, how then do you think your significant other will treat you when things circle around? Most likely it will make them feel loved unconditionally, and it will motivate them to want to treat you the same way when you make a mistake. This type of unconditional love is what every single person longs for in this life. One of the main reasons I believe the divorce rate is so high today is because there is a lack of unconditional love at the center of our relationships. Try loving this kind of way and see where life takes you.

This kind of unconditional love is actually impossible to be able to give. That is, it is impossible to give on your own. Our human nature makes us want to respond back to pain and hurt with those exact same things. Only with Jesus can one truly experience pain and hurt, while choosing to give back love. This response can't actually occur without it being part of your nature. Most people know that when someone gets mad at them, or hurts them, that the best thing to do is to forgive them and to respond back with love and kindness. Actually being able to live that out when you are in the heat of the moment is a whole other thing.

Any pressure type of situation is going to squeeze out our true nature. Most people when they are in this situation respond back with anything but love. Believe me, I lived the majority of my life doing this exact thing. There is only one way to be able to break this cycle and meet hurt, pain, and disappointment with love. That is by allowing Jesus to live on the inside of you. The more He lives on the inside of you, the more you will reflect His nature. In actuality, He already fully lives on the inside of you in your spirit. But your heart, mind, and soul might not fully contain His essence. This is exactly why the Bible tells us to renew our mind. The more we make room in those three areas for Jesus to live, the more He will move in and take up residence.

If our hearts are broken from a past relationship, or our mind is occupied with pain and hurt, then Jesus has no access to come in. That is why it is vital for us to give Jesus our brokenness, and our pain, so that He can move into those areas. If you hold onto unresolved pain in your mind, that is, in your emotional state section of your mind, then Jesus can't come in and live. Jesus' nature is love, joy, peace, etc... So if you hold onto contrary emotions in your emotional state section of your mind, they will take the place of joy, peace, and love. If you don't have those Godly emotions residing in the areas of your heart, mind, and soul, then when someone close to you interacts with you on that level, they are going to experience the emotions that are in there over the course of time. Hence, this is why so many people have a hard time experiencing disappointment from their partner. This is why most people end up only being able to offer conditional forms of love in their relationships.

In order to be able to respond to disappointment with unconditional love, the emotions of love, joy, and peace must be residing in our hearts, souls, and minds. This also applies to our subconscious and conscious minds as well. The only way we can expect to have the fruit of love, joy, peace, etc…, in those areas of our lives, is to exchange the damaging emotions that we don't want with Jesus. One of the most common things people hold in their minds and hearts is the hurt and pain experienced over their lifetime. That is, the times they were wrongly and unjustly treated. Holding onto these experiences causes the initial wound that was formed to get deeper and deeper. Over the course of time, this unresolved pain gets pushed deeper into our subconscious. As you saw in the book, it affects our ability to love and believe. This unresolved pain will not go away until the proper release is applied. This proper release being the process I described throughout this book. Once you decide you want to release these painful wounds from your life, you will begin experiencing the fruit of transformation.

You will experience a sense of peace, love, and joy like you have never tasted before. You will experience feeling whole, complete, valued, and loved. This sensation will then start changing everything around you. You will find yourself breaking the pain cycle I talked about earlier, and you will find yourself on this new cycle of love.

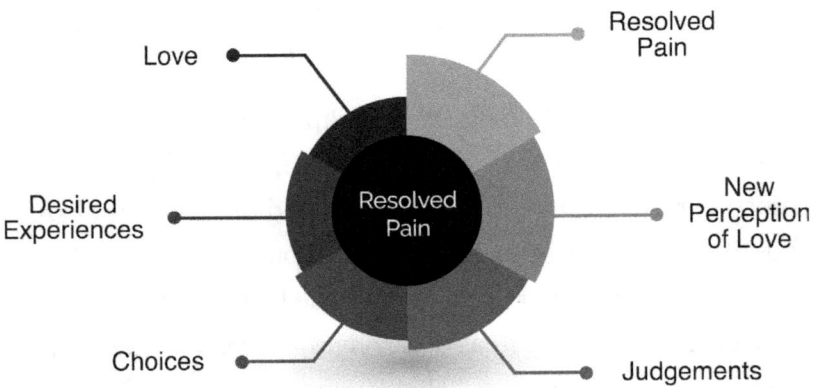

With this newfound nature you will be able to actually do what you knew to do before, but couldn't actually live it out. This ability will then allow you to transform every area of your life, including your closest relationships. The people who were once used to you giving them hurt for hurt will now see something different about you. Your significant other will notice a change. Or if you are single, you will notice that in your next relationship you will be able to receive and give love like you never had before. Since Jesus moved in and resides in more areas of your being, you will reflect more of His nature, and you will see your life producing more of His fruit. You will find yourself not having to deal with the same addictions, pitfalls, and problems that you used to. Like I said, you will find every facet of your life being transformed. But unless you have His nature inside of you, you will be stuck going around and around on the cycle of pain with no way of hopping off. An individual's life will always reflect what is going on at the core. If there is pain and hurt, then their life will have lots of pain and hurt. If there is love and freedom, then their life will have lots of love and freedom. Someone's experiences and behavior is always a reflection of their identity. It's impossible to mask ones behaviors without changing their identity. An apple tree can't grow pears, and a pear tree can't grow apples. If you see yourself as dirty, no good, and worthless, then you are going to experience things that line up with that belief. If you see yourself as righteous, loveable, complete, valued, and whole, then you are going to experience things that line up with that belief.

In closing, this ability to take pain, whether intentional or not, and not let it change who you are, and how you are going to respond, has the ability to revolutionize the world. That's what true God kind of love is. The ability to take any hurtful situation, and not let it stay with you, but to let it go through forgiveness, makes an individual virtually unstoppable. Without the processes I talked about in this book, and without fully understanding Jesus, I believe this ability is physically impossible, since Jesus and true forgiveness confirm your true identity. It's time we allow Jesus to have the entirety of our hearts, minds, and souls. It's time we acknowledge and give Jesus all that He died and paid for. This includes not just our sins, but our iniquities as well. You holding onto them only rob Him of what is rightfully His. The ability to get off of the devastating effects of the pain cycle and jump on over to the love cycle is what true transformation is. It is what true unconditional love is. It is the only place where you can find your true identity, and see yourself the correct way. Where do you wish to reside?

CAN GOD LOVE YOU

I search, never finding
I wait, never being seen

I stop looking, but nothing can be found
I wait, waiting to be found

I repeat, going crazy in this never ending cycle
I wait, looking to be seen

I wish, wishing I could find
I hope, wanting to be seen

I lose hope, seeing that I never find
I love, unconditional of you

I see, did I find?
I love you...

I love you...
How can this be?

I've always loved you...
How can you love me?

I've always loved you...
Why?

Why can I not?
Because......

My love is my choice!
...

I love you my beloved!
...I searched, but never found!!! I stopped looking, but nothing found me!!!...

Yes
...I wished, but never found!!! I lost hope, but nothing found me!!!...

Here I am!!!
I do not understand?

I found you. I didn't need your searching, your looking, your wishing, your hoping
What then do you need?

I need your receiving
How do I do that?

You are speaking to me right now aren't you?
...yes...

Well just believe...
...okay...

Do you believe?
Believe what?

What I told you?
What did you tell me?

I told you I love you, I've always loved you
Yes I remember. That's when I asked why

Correct. I love you my beloved
...

Do you want to continue to ask why?
Not anymore!!!

Can I show you and teach you HOW I love you?
???

Can He???

END NOTES

1. *The Merriam-Webster Thesaurus*, s.v. "complete."

2. *Random House Compact Unabridged Dictionary*, 2nd ed., s.v. "transformation."

3. *Dictionary.com Unabridged*, s.v. "mind", accessed July 27, 2015, http://dictionary.reference.com/browse/mind

4. *Random House Compact Unabridged Dictionary*, 2nd ed., s.v. "sin."

5. *Webster's Third New International Dictionary*, s.v. "sin."

6. *Random House Compact Unabridged Dictionary*, 2nd ed., s.v. "iniquity."

7. *Mathew* 17:24-27.

8. *NIV Study Bible* (Grand Rapids: Zondervan, 2011), 1645.

9. *The American Heritage Dictionary of the English Language*, 4th ed., s.v. "chastise."

10. John 14:6.

11. Mathew 19:26.

12. Colossians 2:15

www.ingramcontent.com/pod-product-compliance
Lightning Source LLC
LaVergne TN
LVHW051546070426
835507LV00021B/2438